First World War
and Army of Occupation
War Diary
France, Belgium and Germany

15 DIVISION
44 Infantry Brigade
Gordon Highlanders
10th Battalion
4 July 1915 - 12 May 1916

WO95/1938/2

The Naval & Military Press Ltd
www.nmarchive.com
Published in association with The National Archives

Published by

The Naval & Military Press Ltd

Unit 10 Ridgewood Industrial Park,

Uckfield, East Sussex,

TN22 5QE England

Tel: +44 (0) 1825 749494

www.naval-military-press.com

www.nmarchive.com

This diary has been reprinted in facsimile from the original. Any imperfections are inevitably reproduced and the quality may fall short of modern type and cartographic standards.

© **Crown Copyright**
Images reproduced by permission of The National Archives, London, England, 2015.

Contents

Document type	Place/Title	Date From	Date To
Heading	WO95/1938 44 Infantry Bde 15 Division 10 Btn Gordon Highlanders July 1915-May 1916		
Heading	15 Division 44 Brigade 10 Bn Gordon Highlanders 1915 July-1916 Apr		
Heading	15th Division. 10th Gordons July 1915 121/3802		
Heading	War Diary of 10th (S) Bn Gordon Highlanders from 4th July 1915 to 30th July 1915		
War Diary	Parkhouse Camp, Salisbury	04/07/1915	08/07/1915
War Diary	Boulogne	09/07/1915	09/07/1915
War Diary	Eperleques	15/07/1915	17/07/1915
War Diary	Houchin	18/07/1915	23/07/1915
War Diary	Les Brebis	24/07/1915	30/07/1915
Miscellaneous	Fighting Strength		
Heading	15th Division 121/0802 10th Gordon Vol II August 1. 15		
War Diary	Les Brebis	01/08/1915	01/08/1915
War Diary	Trenches A/S. Maroc	02/08/1915	10/08/1915
War Diary	Noeux-Les-Mines	13/08/1915	20/08/1915
War Diary	Philosophe	24/08/1915	30/08/1915
Miscellaneous	Fighting Strength		
Heading	44th Inf. Bde. 15th Div. 10th Battn. The Gordon Highlanders. September 1915		
Heading	Reports On Operations 25th/26th September. C.O. Battalion. O.C. "K" Company. M.G.O.		
Miscellaneous	'M' Company report on September 25. 26	25/09/1915	25/09/1915
Miscellaneous	To 44th Brigade	27/09/1915	27/09/1915
Miscellaneous	To Gordon. Narrative of Events on 25th & 26th Sept.	25/09/1915	25/09/1915
Heading	War Diary.		
War Diary	Mazingarbe	01/09/1915	18/09/1915
War Diary	Trenches at X 1 Sector	19/09/1915	30/09/1915
Heading	War Diary of 10th (S) Bn Gordon Highrs from 1st September 1915 to 30th September 1915		
Miscellaneous	G.O.C., 1st Army.	11/09/1915	11/09/1915
Heading	121/7517 10th Gordons October 1915 15th Division.		
War Diary	Houchin	01/10/1915	03/10/1915
War Diary	Lillers	04/10/1915	12/10/1915
War Diary	Noeux	13/10/1915	26/10/1915
War Diary	Trenches	27/10/1915	31/10/1915
Heading	15th Division 10th Gordons November 1915 Vol 5 121/7678		
War Diary	Trenches Sector C. 1	01/11/1915	04/11/1915
War Diary	Reserve Trenches.	05/11/1915	07/11/1915
War Diary	Noeux.	09/11/1915	12/11/1915
War Diary	Noyelles	13/11/1915	15/11/1915
War Diary	Trenches Sector D. 2	16/11/1915	18/11/1915
War Diary	Vermelles	19/11/1915	21/11/1915
War Diary	Trenches Sector D2	22/11/1915	23/11/1915
War Diary	Noeux	24/11/1915	24/11/1915
War Diary	Labourse	26/11/1915	30/11/1915
Heading	121/7909 10th Gordons December 1915 15th Division		

Type	Description	From	To
Heading	War Diary of 10th (S) Bn Gordon Highrs from 1st to 31st December 1915		
War Diary		01/12/1915	08/12/1915
War Diary	Noyelles	10/12/1915	14/12/1915
War Diary	Allouagne	14/12/1915	31/12/1915
Heading	10th Gordons Vol. 7		
Heading	10th Gordons 15. Div Vol. 8		
Heading	January 1916 Diary of 10th (S) Bn Gordon Highlrs		
War Diary	Allouagne	01/01/1916	14/01/1916
War Diary	Mazingarbe	14/01/1916	31/01/1916
Miscellaneous	From Officer Commanding 10th (S) Bn Gordo Highlrs.	05/03/1916	05/03/1916
War Diary	Mazingarbe to Trenches.	01/02/1916	01/02/1916
War Diary	Trenches	02/02/1916	07/02/1916
War Diary	Philosophe	07/02/1916	09/02/1916
War Diary	Philosophe to Trenches	10/02/1916	10/02/1916
War Diary	Trenches	11/02/1916	12/02/1916
Diagram etc	Copy from Sketch	13/02/1916	13/02/1916
War Diary	Trenches to Noeux Les Mines	13/02/1916	13/02/1916
War Diary	Noeux Les Mines	14/02/1916	18/02/1916
War Diary	Noeux Les Mines to Trenches	19/02/1916	19/02/1916
War Diary	Trenches	19/02/1916	27/02/1916
Map	Tracing from Trench Map-Sheet-36c N.W. 3 E2. 6 1/10000 Line Held By Battalion		
War Diary	Trenches	27/02/1916	29/02/1916
Diagram etc	Plan of Fire Trench Held By 10th Gordon Highlanders		
Diagram etc	Plan of Fire Trench Held by 10th Gordon Highlanders.		
Map	Left Sub Section Hulluch Section.		
War Diary			
War Diary		01/02/1916	01/02/1916
Heading	10th Gordons Vol 9		
War Diary	Trenches	01/03/1916	02/03/1916
War Diary	Noeux Les Mines	03/03/1916	06/03/1916
War Diary	Noeux Les Mines to Trenches	07/03/1916	09/03/1916
Diagram etc	Plan of Fire Trench Held By 10th Gordon Highlanders-		
War Diary	Trenches	09/03/1916	16/03/1916
Diagram etc	Tracing from Aeroplane Photo Taken 14/3/16 Map Squares 7.8.13.14.H.		
Diagram etc	Left Sub Section-Hulluch Section		
War Diary		16/03/1916	16/03/1916
War Diary	Trenches	17/03/1916	20/03/1916
War Diary	Noeux Les Mines	20/03/1916	24/03/1916
War Diary	Noeux Les Mines to Allouagne	25/03/1916	27/03/1916
War Diary	Allouagne	28/03/1916	31/03/1916
Heading	Date April 1916 War Diary of 10th (S) Bn Gordon Highrs from 1st to 30th April 1916		
War Diary	Allouagne	01/04/1916	24/04/1916
War Diary	Allouagne to Bethune	25/04/1916	25/04/1916
War Diary	Bethune to Noyelles	26/04/1916	26/04/1916
War Diary	Vermelles & Noyelles	27/04/1916	28/04/1916
War Diary	Vermelles	28/04/1916	28/04/1916
War Diary	Vermelles Noyelles	28/04/1916	30/04/1916
War Diary	Vermelles Noyelles	29/04/1916	29/04/1916
War Diary	Trenches	30/04/1916	30/04/1916
Miscellaneous	Killed in action		
War Diary			

Heading	8/10th (S) Bn Gordon Highrs War Diary 1st to 12th May 1916		
Miscellaneous	From Officer Commanding 11th Entrenching Battalion.	05/06/1916	05/06/1916
War Diary	Trenches	01/05/1916	06/05/1916
Diagram etc	Line occupied by the 10th Gordon Highlanders Riflemans Alley to Swinbourne Loop		
War Diary	Trenches	07/05/1916	10/05/1916
War Diary			
War Diary	Trenches to Bethune	11/05/1916	11/05/1916
War Diary	Bethune	12/05/1916	12/05/1916
War Diary		00/09/1915	00/09/1915
War Diary		00/10/1915	00/10/1915
War Diary		00/11/1915	00/11/1915
War Diary		00/12/1915	00/12/1915
War Diary		00/01/1916	00/01/1916
War Diary		00/02/1916	00/02/1916
War Diary		00/03/1916	00/03/1916
War Diary		00/04/1916	00/04/1916

WO 95/1938

44 INFANTRY BDE

1st DIVISION

10 BTN GORDON HIGHLANDERS

July 1915 – May 1916

15 DIVISION

44 BRIGADE

10 BN GORDON HIGHLANDERS

1915 JULY – 1916 APR

(AMALGAMATED WITH 8 BN
from 9 DIV 26 BDE
To 15 DIV 44 BDE)
KNOWN AS 8/10 BN. FROM 1916 MAY
WITH 44 BDE 15 DIV

10th Gordons.

July 1915.

121/1050

13th Division

10th Gordons
Vol I
July 15

Confidential

War Diary
—— of ——
10th (S) Bn Gordon Highlanders
from
4th July 1915 to 30th July 1915

WAR DIARY
or
INTELLIGENCE SUMMARY.
(Erase heading not required.)

Army Form C. 2118.

Instructions regarding War Diaries and Intelligence Summaries are contained in F. S. Regs., Part II. and the Staff Manual respectively. Title pages will be prepared in manuscript.

Place	Date	Hour	Summary of Events and Information	Remarks and references to Appendices
Parkhouse Camp, Salisbury	July 4 1915	12 noon	Orders to proceed to France on 8th July received	
Do	7		Advance party including transport proceeded under Major H.P. Wallace 2nd Lieut S.B.G. Mackenzie in charge of transport and Lieut J.D. Lammie, to Tidworth Station and thence by train to Southampton and steamer to Havre.	
Do	8	4.30pm	Battalion entrained at Tidworth to Folkestone and embarked at 11.30pm on SS Victoria	
Boulogne	9	1am	Landed at Boulogne. Evening good. Marched to Rest Camp. 8.10am marched from Rest Camp to Pont-de-Brique Station and proceeded in train containing Advance Party to Watten Station. 2.30pm detrained at Watten Station, and marched to Billets at Eperlecques.	
Eperlecques			Battalion remained at Eperlecques until 15th	
Do	15	6.20am	Battalion marches out of Eperlecques and passes starting point of Brigade at Moulle at 6.50am. Route - St Omer, Arques, Renescure, Wallon Cappel to Cnq Rues where Batn. bivouacs at outskirts of Hazebrouck	
	16	6.30am	Batn. marches out of bivouac and proceeds via Morbecque, St Venant, Busnes to billets at Gonnehem	
	17	9pm	Batn. marches out of billets and proceeds by night via Chocques, Fouquieres, Drouvin to	

Geo. H. Gunning

WAR DIARY or INTELLIGENCE SUMMARY.

Army Form C. 2118.

Place	Date	Hour	Summary of Events and Information	Remarks and references to Appendices
Houchin	July 18		to Houchin, where billets were only obtainable for small portion of Battn – the remainder bivouaced	
	19.	1 am	Arrived at Houchin. Orders received the C.O. Adjutant and 5 Sgts go into trenches in Y sector at Vermelles on evening of 20th for two days and then into W sector at Maroc for two days. Also I & K Companies go into trenches at W1 sector on evening of 20th for two days and J & M Coys at same sector the following two days and seconds in Commands, Ameluse Green Officers and 5 Sgts to proceed on 28th July for same tour as C.O., Adjutant and 5 Sgts above mentioned.	
	20.		C.O. Adjutant & 5 Sgts proceed to trenches in Y sector and I & K Coys at 4.40 pm to trenches in W1 sector attached to 9th London Regiment	
	21.		C.O. Lt. Col. Stewart MacDougall killed in action at 11.30 am in trenches by a shell which also mortally wounded Major Forbes 9th K.O.S.B.s and wounded one other officer. Lt. Col. MacDougall's body brought back to Houchin about 12 midnight No S/5482 Pte. Briggs (K Coy) slightly wounded by fragment of shell	
	22.		J & M Coys proceeded to take the place of I & K Coys in W1 sector attached to 21st	

Geo. Shrewsbury Lieut
2nd Lieut

1577 Wt. W10701/1773 500,000 1/15 D. D. & L. A.D.S.S./Forms/C. 2118.

Army Form C. 2118.

WAR DIARY
or
INTELLIGENCE SUMMARY.
(Erase heading not required.)

Instructions regarding War Diaries and Intelligence Summaries are contained in F. S. Regs., Part II. and the Staff Manual respectively. Title pages will be prepared in manuscript.

Place	Date	Hour	Summary of Events and Information	Remarks and references to Appendices
	July		21st London Regiment. Adjutant & 5 Sgts left Y sector and proceeded to W sector	
	23	1.30am	I & K Coys returned to Honchin from trenches at W1 sector.	
		9.30pm	Funeral of Lt. Col. S. MacDougall to Honchin Cemetery.	
ZesBrebia	24	4.15pm	I & K Coys proceeded from Honchin to trenches at Zea Brebia. Lt. M Coys left trenches at W1 and gund remainder of Bahr in trenches at Zea Brebia. Bahr remained at Zea Brebia until 27th August	
	28		Major H. R. Wallace Machine Gun Officer (2nd Lieut. L. W. Gordon) and 5 Sgts proceeded to trenches in Y sector for two days.	
	30		Officers & NCOs. returns to on 28 inst left trenches at Y sector and proceeded to trenches at W sector.	
			Copy of weekly fighting strength Returns appended hereto.	

FIGHTING STRENGTH

Date.	Officers	N.C.O's and men.
1915.		
16th July	29.	1005.
23/7/15.	28.	1004.
30/7/15.	28.	1004.

10th Gordons.

August 1915.

15th Division

10th Gordons
Vol II
August 15

Army Form C. 2118.

WAR DIARY
or
INTELLIGENCE SUMMARY.
(Erase heading not required.)

Instructions regarding War Diaries and Intelligence Summaries are contained in F. S. Regs., Part II and the Staff Manual respectively. Title pages will be prepared in manuscript.

Place	Date	Hour	Summary of Events and Information	Remarks and references to Appendices
Les Brebis	1915 Aug 1		Major Wallace, Machine Gun Officer & 5 NCOs returned from trenches to Les Brebis. Lieut J.D. Lamour admitted to hospital (sick)	
Lynde at S. Marie	2	8pm	Batn. marched to South Maroc & took over trenches at W2 sector from 22nd London Regt	
	3		Snipers active	
	4		Snipers active. No 5/5088 Pte Auckland and No 5/5615 Pte Hogan accidentally wounded	
	5		Snipers more active. No 3/6802 Sgt McLaren wounded by shrapnel. 5/6481 Pte Young wounded by sniper and No 5/4762 Pte McQuoky accidentally wounded	
	6		Trench duties. Threw a large quantity of material for into Cookers in Mine Yard which caused a large volume of smoke. Enemy immediately bombarded Mine Yard & L/Cpl Robertson slightly wounded by fragment of shell. Civilian arrested & sent under escort to Brigade H.Qrs.	
	8		Cpl Melton (X Coy) killed while on patrol during night. He was buried at 10pm at Maroc Church.	
	9		Snipers active. Enemy shells opening craters & wood piles for 20 minutes in afternoon. No damage done. Our Artillery retaliated	
	10		Relieved by 8" K.O.S.B. and proceeds to Billets at Noeux-les-Mines	

Geo A. Lamsden
Lt Col

Army Form C. 2118.

WAR DIARY
or
INTELLIGENCE SUMMARY.
(Erase heading not required.)

Instructions regarding War Diaries and Intelligence Summaries are contained in F. S. Regs., Part II. and the Staff Manual respectively. Title pages will be prepared in manuscript.

Place	Date	Hour	Summary of Events and Information	Remarks and references to Appendices
Noeux-les-Mines	Aug. 3		The following appeared in this day's Batn. Routine Orders:- "124. Commands &c. The following extract from the Supplement to the London Gazette dated 11th August is published for information. "Infantry, Service Battalion. 10th London Highlanders. Temporary Major J.R. Wallace to command the Battalion and to be temporary Lieut-Colonel (July 22nd)." "Battalion vice Major J.R. Wallace promoted. Authority - W.O. letter No. 100/8d/1501/Y. M.S.K. of 3.8.15."	
	16		L/Cpl. and 3 men sent to form nucleus of Gas Corps.	
	17		Cpl. Dickson accidentally shot in stomach by the French.	
	18	7.30pm	Left Noeux-les-Mines & proceeded to billets at Mazingarbe.	
	19	8 pm	Left Mazingarbe for billets Philosophe.	
	20		Sgt. Norton (L Coy) wounded whilst out with working party, died in hospital at Noeux-les-Mines and buried in Cemetery near Noeux-les-Mines Station.	

Geo. Hermady
2nd Lieut.

Army Form C. 2118.

WAR DIARY
or
INTELLIGENCE SUMMARY.
(Erase heading not required.)

Instructions regarding War Diaries and Intelligence Summaries are contained in F. S. Regs., Part II. and the Staff Manual respectively. Title pages will be prepared in manuscript.

Place	Date	Hour	Summary of Events and Information	Remarks and references to Appendices
Philosophe	Aug. 24		Enemy put six shells (shrapnel) at and near Cross Roads. No damage done.	
	25		Enemy shelled Fosse No 3 in forenoon. Lieut Harper admitted to hospital (sick).	
	26	2.30pm	Battalion left Philosophe and relieves 7th Cameron Highlanders in trenches at X 2.	
	28.	3 pm	Capt R.G. Longman wounded in thigh and abdomen by bullet whilst reconnoitering ground in front of our fire trench.	
	30		Relieved by 6th Cameron Highlanders and proceeds to fields at Mazingarbe. First Draft consisting of Lieut. C.G. Hallard and 48 other ranks arrived.	
			Copy of weekly fighting Strength Returns appended hereto.	

Geo J Humston
2nd Lieut

FIGHTING STRENGTH

Date	Officers	N.C.O's and men.
6/8/15.	28.	999.
13/8/15.	28.	989.
20/8/15.	28.	978.
27/8/15.	27.	979.

44th Inf.Bde.
15th Div.

10th BATTN. THE GORDON HIGHLANDERS.

S E P T E M B E R

1 9 1 5

Attached:

Reports on Operations
25th/26th September:
  C.O. Battalion.
  O.C. "K" Company.
  M.G.O.

REPORTS ON OPERATIONS 25TH/26TH SEPTEMBER.

C.O. Battalion.
O.C. "K" Company.
M.G.O.

COPY.

'M' Company report on September 25, 26.

A number of men were gassed right at the beginning, and in trying to avoid the gassed bays the two front platoons were separated before leaving the trenches. One party under Lieut.Boyd joined on to some 9th Gordon's and were with the Black Watch when they charged the first line trenches. The other party under Sergt.Aitken reported to L Coy. but later joined on to the 2 rear platoons of M Company under Lieut. Robertson. This party carried right on through Loos and on to Hill 70 without much loss. When they crossed the crest of Hill 70, they found several machine guns in action and a line of K.O.S.B. on their left. They joined up and advanced down the hill. There seemed to be some doubt as to whether there was any of our own troops in front. Suddenly they found a strong line of barbed wire concealed in the grass and at the same time a heavy machine gun and rifle fire was opened on them. They lay down and tried to make some cover. Lieut.Robertson was the only officer left. The party was about 600 strong of different regiments. Various attempts were made to communicate back. Sergt. Cavers got up under a heavy fire and signalled back for support with platoon flags, but he was soon hit. Sergt.Aitken and Pte.Mc.Keller crawled back and the former reached O.C. 7th Camerons who was digging in on reverse slope of Hill 70. Pte.Davidson also went back with a message, None of these attempts produced any result, and the line had to retire as the enemy were getting round the right flank. They retreated to reverse slope of Hill 70 where they held on till early next morning when they were relieved.

M.Company. Sergt.Aitken (taken in shorthand)

When we started away from the front line No 3 and 4 sections got through one of the bays where there was gas and some of our men got gassed there and had to turn back and come through the support trench. We went round the support trench and we came to the rear of L Company where I reported I had lost connection with Mr Boyd. Capt.Angus told me just to attach ourselves to the rear of the company, and when we got into the open to rejoin Mr Boyd. When we got into the open we were in the rear of L Company and Major Crichton instructed me to keep to the left as we had to go on to support the Camerons. On making to the left I met Lieut.Robertson and about two platoons of our Company and joined in with the line. Lieut.Robertson was the only officer in command of that line. The left of our line was in connection with the 7th K.O.S.B.

We advanced in an extended line right on to Loos Village and when we were coming near the village the whole line took a left incline and passed the left hand side of the village. We advanced right over the moor on to Hill 70 and some officer told us that the Camerons and Black Watch were occupying the village in front and we pushed over to support them.

When we got over the crest we found a number of machine guns firing on men in front. Lieut.Christison joined our line and instructed the machine gunners to stop firing, as they were firing on the Black Watch and Camerons. We then proceeded down the hill towards the village in front when a murderous machine gun and rifle fire opened on us. Instead of it being the Black Watch and Camerons as we thought, we found it to be the retreating enemy who ran down a road through houses and manned a trench heavily barbed wired.

We advanced until we were about 150 yards from this trench and Lieut.Robertson, who was in command of the line, gave orders for the men to make head cover. The enemy's fire was causing a great deal of casualties on the line. I was there over two hours when Lieut. Robertson asked for volunteers to go back with a message to Major Crichton. Mc.Keller and myself went back and reported to Colonel Sandelands what was happening in front. Mc.Kellar was wounded on the way up. I found Colonel Sandelands with men digging themselves in on the reverse slope of Hill 70. When we were in the advanced line I saw Sergt.Cavers signalling back for reinforcements.

(signed) Hugh Aitken, Sergt.

Corpl. Simin.

We were about 2 or 3 hours after Sergt. Aitken left under a heavy machine gun and rifle fire on our right flank, which caused us to retire to the crest of Hill 70 where we held the position until relieved

In the advanced position, L/C Turner and Pte. Lund were bombing a keep on the left flank next the road and when the company retired, were cut off. They duly retired under a heavy fire and after they had cleared out the keep.

(Signed) W. Simin, Cpl.

To:-
44th Brigade   E

7-25 pm. 27th Sept.

I have received instructions to send in a short account of the part taken by my unit in the recent action, from the start on the morning of 25th until the night of the 26th.

On the morning of 25th the advance of the 44th Brigade commenced as prearranged according to time, and without a hitch.

At 7.45 am I issued orders, in accordance with instructions from the 44th Brigade, at the moment when my leading platoon was advancing over the parapet to consolidate as far forward as possible behind the 9th Cameron.

I left the parapet with my Adjutant and Signalling Officer and HQ Company immediately behind my last platoon, and on reaching a point in the

German support trench at about
G.28.C.9.2. I came up with Col:
Sandilands of the 7th Camerons
and ascertained from him that
he was advancing from that point
in the direction of LOOS CHURCH
which he proceeded to do. It appeared
to me however that at this point
the general line of advance was
more to the north west corner of
LOOS, and I followed that line, which
turned out to be, as I anticipated,
the general line of the advance.
     I came up with O.C. "M" Coy.
(the left rear Company) at about
G.29.C.5.0 who explained to me
the route which his platoons had
taken bearing right-handed through
the village of LOOS. Major Crichton
(the officer in question) asked me at
what point he could send back
information when he had
cleared LOOS, and I said as far
as possible in rear of some small
haystacks at the point above named.
After waiting for some time I
joined the general advance of the
attack, together with the Machine
Gun Section of the 9th Gordons

in the direction of HILL 70 to the point A.31.c central, where I came up with Major Rankin Campbell of the Royal Scots Fusiliers, 46th Bde. who informed me that the unit had become mixed at this point as well as the Brigades. I conferred with him and we agreed to consolidate, which we did, and continued the advance to the top of HILL 70 where we were held up by a very heavy machine gun fire for upwards of three quarters of an hour. There were several retirements on our left which we rallied at A.31.a.5.0 southwestwards towards the CRASSIER. Here I discovered on my right Col. Sandilands of the 7th Camerons rallying that part of the line which was extending from our right towards the CRASSIER. I conferred with him as to what should be done, and acting upon his instructions, with which I agreed, we consolidated the line and dug in. I sent back a report to Bde. HQ stating the position at about 12.30 pm and asking for tools, as progress was slow and difficult with entrenching tools only. At this point Colonel Sandilands also issued orders for the units in the firing line to retire upon him the attack on CITE ST AUGUSTE having for the moment failed on account of the barbed wire at this point not having been cut.

The remnants of the units comprising the 44th, 45th & 46th Brigades remained in this position throughout the greater part of the night.

I received instructions that on relief by units of the 62nd Brigade I was to proceed to the GRENAY-VERMELLES line or PHILOSOPHE whichever was most convenient, and which I proceeded to do at 3.30 a.m. 26th.

On the 26th as instructed by the Brigadier I brought up the remainder of my battalion from GRENAY-VERMELLES line to QUALITY STREET, there to stand-by under his orders, and during the forenoon we proceeded to occupy that portion of our own trenches in X.1. from 5a to Sap 8 with the remnants of the other units of the Brigade.

Later in the evening I received orders to occupy the section of the German support trenches nearest LOOS from G.34.a.6.5 to G.28.a.3.7 which in conjunction with Col. Sandilands of the 7th Camerons I immediately proceeded to do. I remained in this position until ordered to move to MAZINGARBE at 3 am 29th inst.

I extremely regret that I have been unable to send in this hurried report at the time specified owing to the hour at which the message was received.

Hugh R Wallace
Lt-Colonel
Comm'd'g 10th Gordon H'rs

Reports from Captain I.G. Thom and 2nd Lieut F.W. Gordon attached.

Report by Capt J.G Thom on the action in
the vicinity of Loos on Sept 25th - 26th

My company as ordered followed the
Cameron Highlanders. We moved off at
6.40 AM & reached Loos at 7 AM. Here
there was a good deal of street & house to
house fighting & whilst the bombing
squads did good work in Loos the
units taking part in the attack were
disorganised - but all the men were
collected in the open ground east of the
village and a new firing line was
formed which advanced up Hill 70.
We were then in touch with the
London Division on our right.
Eventually this mixed firing line
— the left of which had advanced
over the hill & down towards the
Cité del Auguste & then had been forced to
retire — dug itself in on the western
slope of Hill 70 between Loos & the crest.
This line was held & several
attacks by the Germans were repulsed
At Dawn on the 26th I received instructions
from Capt Longman that I was
to be relieved by a company of
the Northumberland Fusiliers & that

17.

I was to retire. The relief however was never effected. & so I held on in the hope of being able to retire when the 62nd Brigade attacked in the morning. The attack was unsuccessful however & we still held on our part of the line & aided in rallying the Northumberland Fusiliers who were retreating. On the left flank to the trench of the 62nd Brigade did retire considerably & at one time — about 10 A.M. on the 26th a force of Germans succeeded in getting into Loos — They were soon after driven out.

About 12 noon — I discovered that the Officer Commanding the Northumberland Fusiliers had ordered his men to retire. I therefore ordered my men to retire by small parties to Quality Street where I collected them. During the retiral I found that the East Yorkshire Regiment — which was to support the Northumberland Fusiliers — but who had promised to enforce when called on — had retired without informing the firing line.

W Thom Capt
OC R Co

To Gordon.

Narrative of events on 25th & 26th Sept.

On the afternoon of Sept. 24th I attached each of the four machine guns under my command to a company of the battalion. The two guns with "L" and "M" companies advanced with them on the right of the Lens Road each under the charge of a sergeant. The two guns attached to "I" and "K" companies advanced from Trench 24 on the left or north side of the Lens Road.

All the machine guns advanced through Loos, where several casualties occurred, and pushed on up the slope of Hill 70 beyond. Nos 1 & 4 guns attached to L and M companies went over the crest and down the other side of the hill along with the greater part of their

2.

companies and a mixed force of Black Watch, Cameron & Seaforths. Here they came under a very heavy enfilade fire from their left where the enemy had a strong point or keep surrounded by barbed wire, just in front of the Cité du St. Auguste. Eventually after suffering heavy casualties the whole line had to retire thro' our second line which was lying on the crest of the hill and took up a position on the far side of the hill where it began to dig itself in. During this retirement one of the two machine guns was lost through the No.1 becoming a casualty and falling. He was rather behind the others at the time and apparently nobody noticed him fall. Just before this occurred the gun had been temporarily put of action. The other gun was successfully extricated. Both did a lot of firing when on the German position at Cité de St Auguste before it was seen that the position we had taken up was really quite untenable.

Meanwhile the other two guns (Nos. 2 and 3) had been lying on the brow of the hill with the second line, which was also a composite force of Gordons, Camerons, Seaforths and Black Watch. No. 2 gun was under myself, and No. 3 gun further to the left under Sergeant Shaw. For fear of hitting our own men we did not open overhead fire from this position. The whole of the second line waited until the first line had passed through it and then also retired to the same line

4.

as the latter took up, on the Xs
side of the hill. Both lines retired under heavy fire, & then dug in.

During the remainder of the
day (Sat). the enemy left our new
line comparatively unmolested. Enemy snipers appeared to be crawling
about the long grass on the top of the
hill. During the night and early
morning however they made repeat-
ed attempts to get ~~across~~ attack our
left flank and my own gun and
Sgt. Shaw's were firing nearly all
the time. This and bursts of rapid
rifle fire succeeded in holding
them off. The two Vickers guns of
the Motor Machine Gun Section
on our right flank protected us on
the side of the slag heap. They
were also engaged nearly all
night, as the enemy kept trying to

45

work down the railway cutting on the slag heap. In my opinion we were absolutely saved by the help given us by these two guns.

During the morning of Sunday 26th Sept. Sgt. Shaw's gun was relieved along with all "C" Coy. The ~~Lancashire~~ Northumberland Fusiliers made a heavy attack on the enemy during the morning. This was a failure as the left of the line retired, leaving the right more or less in the air.

Eventually the whole line on the hill was given up by the order of the O.C. the Battⁿ of Northumberland Fusiliers and my only remaining gun team of 4 men and myself retired with our gun and re-assembled at Quality Street.

86.

No. 4 gun (attached to M" Coy) was relieved on the Sunday morning after doing good work.

Sgt. Shaw's gun was totally out of action by the time it was relieved as a bullet penetrated the body, and my own was firing very badly, at the end.

My gun team disabled a German Maxim on Hill 70 by removing the lock and shooting down the barrel.

I would like to mention the following N.C.Os and men for the specially good work they did, though it is almost impossible to pick out individuals where all were so excellent. The courage & perseverance of the whole section was magnificent and the work that they did was invaluable.

%:-

Sgt. Lo Burns (killed)
" G. Shaw
L/Cpl. Martin (wounded)
" Masson
Pte Ferrans
" Ritchie (wounded)

Geo. Gordon
2nd Lieut.
W90. 10th Gordon High'rs

WAR DIARY.

INTELLIGENCE SUMMARY.

(Erase heading not required.)

10th GORDON HIGHRS.

Place	Date	Hour	Summary of Events and Information	Remarks and references to Appendices
MAZINGARBE	1915 Sept 1			
Do	2			
	3		Orders received that 1 Officer, and 1 N.C.O. and 7 men from one platoon of each Company proceed to bombing course commencing 5th inst at NOEUX-LES-MINES	
	4		2nd Lieut Husband and 32 other ranks proceeded to NOEUX-LES-MINES for above course	
	5			
	6		Batn. Bombing Officer (2nd Lieut Inglis) and 2nd Lieut Wood proceeded to G.H.Q. to inspect german grenades.	
	7		Batn. Machine Gun Sections proceeded to trenches at X1 Sector.	
		1:30 pm	Batn. moves into GRENAY Line Trenches (Second line advance trenches). – Batn. H.Q.s. remaining at MAZINGARBE.	
	8		L and M Coys. returned from GRENAY line trenches to MAZINGARBE	
	9		L and M Coys. proceeds from MAZINGARBE to trenches extending from G.20.c.5.6. to G.26.A.5.0. (GRENAY Line VERMELLES BRANCH Trench.	
	10		I and SK Coys returned from GRENAY line trenches to MAZINGARBE	

Ing M Callum Lt Colonel
10th Gordon Highrs.

INTELLIGENCE SUMMARY.

(Erase heading not required.)

10th GORDON HIGHRS.

Place	Date	Hour	Summary of Events and Information	Remarks and references to Appendices
MAZINGARBE	Sept 11			
	12.		Machine Gun Section returns to MAZINGARBE from trenches at X1 Sector. No S/4992 L/Cpl Wyganos and S/7098 Pte Weir M'Coy wounds by premature explosion of a shell.	
	13.		I & K Coys relieves L and M Coys who returns to MAZINGARBE.	
	14.		First line Transport moves from VERQUIN to NOEUX-LES-MINES.	
	15.			
	16.		L and M Coys relieves I & K Coys who returns to MAZINGARBE.	
	17.		No S/5651 Pte McPherson "L" Coy wounds by Shrapnel.	
	18.			
Trenches at X1 Sector.	19	12 noon	Batn. relieves 13th ROYAL SCOTS in X1 Sector, extending from G.34.A.0.1 to G.28.A.5.2.	
	20.		Enemy landed a few High Explosive and Shrapnel shells & also a few Rifle Grenades. Lieut T.H.B. VADE WALPOLE and No S/10320 Pte Crosbie, No S/5412 L/Cpl Connor and S/5349 Pte Laird 'M'Coy killed in action. No S/5526 Pte Dineo I Coy and S/8252 Pte Elliot M Coy wounded.	
	21	7am	Heavy Artillery Bombardment of enemy wire & trenches commenced and continues throughout day until 6pm. Bombardment continued intermittently during	

A.Y.M. Shakoe, Lt Colonel 10th Gordon Highlrs.

INTELLIGENCE SUMMARY.

(Erase heading not required.)

Place	Date	Hour	Summary of Events and Information	Remarks and references to Appendices
Trenches at X1 Sector	Sept. 21		10th GORDON HIGHRS During night. Enemy retaliated slightly in forenoon with trench mortars and a few High Explosive and Shrapnel shells. During night enemy had two small working parties which were dispersed by machine gun, rifle and artillery fire. No 3/6855 Sgt McCulloch 'M' Coy. killed by dug out being blown in. No S/8458 Pte Gordon. No S/5180 Pte Michie. No S/5619 Pte Hurst, 'I' Coy; No S/5321 Sgt Bant No S/7111 2/Cpl Gauld. No S/5047 Pte Deans 'L' Coy; No S/4220 Pte Disk and No S/9476 Pte Martin 'M' Coy wounded.	
	22		Intermittent bombardment of enemy's position continued until 9 am. when heavy bombardment re-commenced and continued throughout day until 6 pm, thereafter intermittent bombardment. Enemy again retaliated slightly with trench mortars, H.E. and shrapnel shells, doing slight damage to our trenches No S/5321 Sgt Bant wounded yesterday died of wounds. Nos S/5018 Pte Lang S/3519 2/Cpl Coleman, S/5012 Pte Kaine, S/4490 Pte Bowman, S/10744 Pte Evans, 'I' Coy; S/4664 Pte Raine and S/5359 Pte Grant 'M' Coy wounded MyhWallace Lt Colonel 10th Gordon Highrs	

INTELLIGENCE SUMMARY.

(Erase heading not required.)

Place	Date	Hour	Summary of Events and Information	Remarks and references to Appendices
Trenches at Ri Siech	Sept 23		**10th GORDON HIGHRS** Intermittent Artillery bombardment until 9 am, thereafter artillery continued the heavy bombardment as on 21st and 22nd until 3.55 pm when Artillery opened intense fire on enemy's front trenches. At 4 pm Artillery lifts on to second line and at 4.3 pm back to front line trenches. From 4 to 4.3 pm Batn manned our front line trenches, shewed their bayonets and cheered with the object to induce the enemy to think an attack was imminent and so man their trenches before Artillery came back at 4.3 pm to front line trenches. From 4.3 pm to 6 pm bombardment continued as previously, thereafter intermittent bombardment during night. The following casualties occurred during the day:- Killed. No S/2254 Pte Garscadden, K Coy. 3/6864 Pte Dillon "L" Coy. 3/6825 Sgt Mitchell S/6836 Sgt Robertson, S/4882 Pte Leeo, S/4940 Pte Beattie, S/4954 Pte McLean, S/4233 Pte Hamilton. Wounded. S/5174 Pte Gibb, I Coy. S/5115 Pte Peacock, S/8090 Pte McDonald. S/5431 Pte Eliot, K Coy, 3/6859 S/7121 Pte Sharkey, I Coy. S/5399 Pte Smith. S/5391 Pte Cowan, S/7221 Pte Stirling, S/7102 Pte Berry S/4665 Pte Leggatt, S/4697 2/Cpl Cowper M Coy + S/5664 Pte Thomson. I Coy. Pte Grant noted as wounded, died of wounds. Hugh Wallace. Lt Colonel, 10th Gordon Highrs.	

INTELLIGENCE SUMMARY.

(Erase heading not required.)

Summaries are contained in F. S. Regs., Part II and the Staff Manual respectively. Title pages will be prepared in manuscript.

Place	Date	Hour	Summary of Events and Information	Remarks and references to Appendices
Trenches at X1 sector.	Sept 23	10 P.M.	**10th Gordon Highrs** Between 10 P.M. and midnight diagonal lanes were cut through the barbed wire in front of bays 61, 64, 67, 70, 73, 76, 79, 82, 85, 88, 91, 94, 97, 100, 103, 106 all north of LENS road. Between the firing line and support both north and south of LENS road the wire was rolled up into heaps. Patrols were sent out by I, L, and M companies and reported the enemy were well cut up and many working parties in their support line.	
	24	2 P.M.	Intermittent bombardment all morning. At 2 P.M. enemy opened rapid rifle and bombarded our lines with shrapnel; some Verey lights were sent up from their support line. The men stood to in their dug outs. Sergt Major Morrison was killed and one man was wounded. In the evening the battalion was relieved north of LENS road by the 9th BLACK WATCH and 8th SEAFORTHS, and north of bryan 5 by the 9th GORDON'S.	
		6.45 P.M.	At 6.45 P.M. two men for each of the following bays were detailed by L and M companies as candle holders under the orders of special company R.E. ;— 4, 7, 10, 19, 22, 26, 30, 33, 36, 40, 41, 44, 46, 50, 52/3, 56, 59.	
		10 P.M.	By 10 P.M. I and K companies were in position in trench 24; L and M companies were in the front two lines from Sap 18 exclusive to bryan 5a.	

J.W. Chalmer
J.W. Chalmer 10th Gordon Hrs.

INTELLIGENCE SUMMARY.

(Erase heading not required.)

Place	Date	Hour	Summary of Events and Information	Remarks and references to Appendices
Sd. ras.			10th Gordon Highrs.	
			Orders for attack:— 1. Objective — (a) German front trench from point of salient in G.34.a.4.9. to the little cross trench at G.28.c.8.6. and the support trench behind the line; (b) the German second line trench from G.35.c.6.3. to G.35.c.4.5.; (c) LOOS village; (d) PUITS No. 15 (HILL 70); (e) German works in H.31.d.; (f) CITE ST AUGUSTE; (g) high ground north of LOISON-sous-LENS.	
			2. Assault. — The assault by the brigade will be delivered in 2 columns. 1st column — 9th BLACK WATCH on the right, 8th SEAFORTHS on the left, each battalion being formed up in depth on a frontage of two platoons; 2nd column — (a) Support Battalion 7th CAMERONS (b) Reserve Battalion 10th GORDONS, each battalion being formed up in depth on a frontage of four platoons.	
	5.50 p.m.		From this time there was a discharge of gas and smoke candles lasting 40 minutes. It was accompanied by a heavy shrapnel bombardment of the enemy first and second lines.	
	6.30 p.m.		At 6.30 A.M. the assaulting columns went over the parapet.	
	6.40 p.m.		At 6.40 our leading companies left the trenches and reached LOOS with slight loss at 7 A.M. Here they had some street fighting and the Londoners	
	7 p.m.		did some good work in the cellars. All units got mixed up in the village, but formed into line again when clear of it. They then	

H.H. Chalmers
Lt. Colonel, 10th Gordon Highrs.

Place	Date	Hour	Summary of Events and Information	Remarks and references to Appendices

Sept 25.

<u>Hill Gordon Heights</u>

11:30 A.M. advanced onto HILL 70 where they established themselves on the reverse slope with the 7th CAMERONS at about 11:30 A.M. "S" I and M companies advanced along with parties of several other units over the crest of HILL 70. They were however held up by strong barbed wire, and a seething machine gun and rifle fire was opened on them. After holding this position for over four hours they were forced to retire over the crest and rejoin the other line late in the afternoon. The position on HILL 70 was held all through the night against constant counter attacks. Two of the machine guns did excellent work on the left of our line. The other two had followed their companies over the crest; one was lost and the other damaged.

26. 3:30 P.M. The battalion was relieved and retired to the VERMELLES–GRENAY line, but parts of K and L companies stayed in the firing line till midday on

VERMELLES-GRENAY

9 A.M. account of a German counter attack. At 9 A.M. the order came to occupy our old front line north of LENS road, and later on to hold the German support line, and the Battalion spent the night here.

In H. Wallace

Lt Colonel 10th Gordon Hdrs

INTELLIGENCE SUMMARY.

(Erase heading not required.)

Place	Date	Hour	Summary of Events and Information	Remarks and references to Appendices
			10th GORDON HIGHRS	
	Sep 27.	2.30 AM.	We were relieved and retired to MAZINGARBE. Our losses during the action were	
			1. Officers wounded Lt WATSON, Lt ROCHE (RAMC), 2nd Lt LUMSDEN, 2nd Lt SYME, 2nd Lt ROBERTSON.	
			2. Officers wounded & missing MAJOR CRICHTON, LT CHRISTISON.	
			3. N.C.O.'s and men. killed 23; wounded 221; wounded & missing 16; missing 114. Total 7 officers, 374 NCO's and men; 1 mule.	
	28.	9.30 AM.	The battalion left MAZINGARBE and proceeded into billets at HOUCHIN.	
	29.		A draft of 48 men arrived. 12 were posted to each company. Casualty returns were checked and refitting was proceeded with.	
	30.		Packs and kits of killed, wounded and missing were despatched.	

MKWallace
Lt Colonel.
10" Gordon Highlanders".

Confidential (Nothing but facts and particulars)

SUMMARY

(will be prepared in manuscript. This Bank Journal throughout the day)

Place	Date	Hour	Summary of events and information	Remarks and references to Appendices

War Diary of 10th Bn Gordon Highrs

10th (S) Bn Gordon High'rs

The Battalion landed at Boulogne on 9th May 1915 & proceeded to billets at Ostrohove. It marched from there on 11th May & arrived at [illegible] on 12th May where it came under orders of 44th Infantry Brigade 15th Division

From 1st September 1915
to 30th September 1915

[signature]
Lt Col
Commanding 10th Bn Gordon Highlanders

SECRET.

> HEADQUARTERS.
> 1 1 SEP. 1915
> No. S. 34
> 44th INFANTRY BRIGADE

I.

G.O.C., 1st Army.

It has come to the notice of the French and British military authorities that cases have occurred where cartridges have been found on enemy prisoners of which the bullets have been tampered with, i.e., the nose cut off or blunted, or the envelope slit; also cartridges have been discovered with the point inwards. It will be made known to officers in command of units that whenever enemy prisoners are found in actual possession of such cartridges three officers will be at once assembled to verify the facts and to record the prisoner's name, regiment, etc. If there is no doubt that the man is in possession of such ammunition, which is a contravention of Appendix 2 of the Hague declaration dated 29th July, 1899, he will be shot at once, the record signed by the officers and the cartridges found on the man being despatched to A.G.G.H.Q.

Care will be taken to discriminate between bullets as above mentioned and those which, although not in conformity with the Hague Declaration, have evidently been issued to the men and have not been tampered with by them. In such cases the blame is with the authority issuing and not with the individual soldier.

Please acknowledge.

G.H.Q. 22.3.15. Sd/ C.F.N.MACREADY, Lt.Gen., Adjt.Gen.

II. 44th Brigade S.G.

O.C. 9th Black Watch.
    8th Seaforths.
    10th Gordons.
    7th Camerons.

For information and necessary action.

Acknowledge.

                Captain,
            for Brigade Major,
            44th Infantry Brigade.

11.9.15.

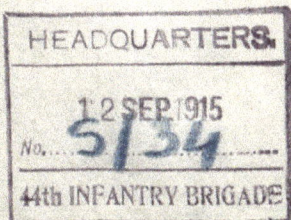

121/7517.

10th Gordons.

October 1915.

15th Division

10th Gordons
Vol: 4

Oct 15.

Army Form C. 2118.

WAR DIARY
or
INTELLIGENCE SUMMARY.
(Erase heading not required.) 10th Batt. Gordon Highlanders

Instructions regarding War Diaries and Intelligence Summaries are contained in F. S. Regs., Part II. and the Staff Manual respectively. Title pages will be prepared in manuscript.

Place	Date	Hour	Summary of Events and Information	Remarks and references to Appendices
HOUCHIN.	Oct 1	10 A.M.	Strength 22 officers, 628 other ranks.	
		10 A.M.	The 44th Inf. Brigade with 9th Battn (Pioneers) GORDON HIGHLANDERS, 73rd Company R.E., was addressed by Sir Henry Rawlinson, G.O.C. II Army Corps.	
	2.	10 A.M.	The battalion was addressed by General McCracken, commanding 15th Division.	
	3.	9.30 A.M.	Orders received to be ready to move at a moment's notice.	
		12 NOON	The brigade left and arrived at LILLERS via BRUAY and LOZINGHEM at 4.30 P.M. There was considerable difficulty about finding billets. A new draft of 50 men under Lieut. Harper arrived.	
LILLERS.	4.		Strength 24 officers, 678 other ranks.	
	5.		Lieut Holland proceeded to ALLOUAGNE for a bombing course. 2nd Lieut Robertson proceeded to BATH for leave, accompanied by 4 other ranks by train leaving LILLERS at 2.30 P.M. Orders for this move were received at 2.10 P.M. 2nd Lieuts Milne and Tulloh reported for duty and were attached to I and L companies respectively.	

Army Form C. 2118.

WAR DIARY
INTELLIGENCE SUMMARY
(Erase heading not required.)

10th Batt. Gordon Highlanders

Instructions regarding War Diaries and Intelligence Summaries are contained in F. S. Regs., Part II. and the Staff Manual respectively. Title pages will be prepared in manuscript.

Place	Date	Hour	Summary of Events and Information	Remarks and references to Appendices
LILLERS.	Oct 6.	9 am	The Battalion went for a route march HAM, MOLINGHEM, BERGUETTE, HAM, LILLERS.	
	7.		2nd Lieuts Shrott and Stewart reported for duty and were attached to K company.	
	8.		The Adjutant and 7 other ranks went on leave.	
	10.	9 a.m.	The battalion went for a route march by L'ECLEME, BUSNES, LE CORNET BOURDOIS. Orders received stopping any further leave. 2nd Lieut G. Robertson and M. Jean reported for duty and were posted to M and L companies.	
	11.		2nd Lt Law reported for duty and was posted to L company. The battalion went for a route march and battalion drill on the road to BERGUETTE.	
	12.	5.30 PM	The 44th Brigade left LILLERS by tram and went into billets at NOEUX-LES-MINES. Orders were given to be ready to march off at short notice.	
NOEUX.	13.		2nd Lt Barr was transferred to this battalion from the 7th Batt. Cameron Highlanders and 2nd Lt Timline was transferred to the latter battalion.	

Army Form C. 2118.

WAR DIARY
~~INTELLIGENCE SUMMARY.~~
(Erase heading not required.)

10th Battn Gordon Highrs

Place	Date	Hour	Summary of Events and Information	Remarks and references to Appendices
NOEUX.	Oct 13.		Orders were given to stand by from midday onwards.	
		9 P.M.	Orders received that men need not stand by, but must be ready to move at a hour's notice.	
	14.		The battalion route-marched to HOUCHIN by companies. From 6 P.M. companies were ready to move off at one hour's notice.	
	15.	10 A.M.	Companies paraded independently for bayonet fighting, company drill etc.	
		2:30.	Route march to HOUCHIN.	
		6 P.M.	Men no longer confined to billets, but must be within earshot of billets in case of alarm.	
	16.		A draft of 20 men returned from hospital, having been wounded or gassed on September 25th. Strength 29 officers, 698 other ranks.	
	17.		Route march thro' DROUVIN and VAUDRICOURT. The Commanding Officer went on leave.	
	18.		Capt Angus and 4 other ranks went on leave. Battalion drill in the afternoon.	

Army Form C. 2118.

WAR DIARY
OF
~~INTELLIGENCE SUMMARY.~~ 4th Battn Gordon Highrs
(Erase heading not required.) 10th Battn Gordon Highrs

Instructions regarding War Diaries and Intelligence Summaries are contained in F. S. Regs., Part II. and the Staff Manual respectively. Title pages will be prepared in manuscript.

Place	Date	Hour	Summary of Events and Information	Remarks and references to Appendices
NOEUX	Oct 19		A draft of 50 men arrived. 20 were posted to S.I., 30 B.M. company. The battalion route marched to VAUDRICOURT.	
		2:30 P.M.	Strength 29 officers, 746 other ranks.	
	20.	2:30.	Route march to HOUCHIN.	
	21.	2:30.	Route march to VAUDRICOURT.	
	23.	7 a.m.	4 officers, 300 other ranks met R.E. guide at PHILOSOPHE for digging in back trenches.	
	24.		The Adjutant, Capt Sutherland, Lt Paterson, Lt Law, Lt Hancock sent over the trenches occupied by 13th Battn The Royal Scots preparatory to taking over from them.	
	25.		The C. in command, officers returned from leave.	
	26.		The battalion took over ones trenches in C.1. area from 13th Battn The Royal Scots	
Trenches	27.		C.1 is part W. of HULLUCH and is in the salient formed by our capture of LOOS. There are old German trenches. Time spent mostly in cleaning & improving trenches and in salvage work. Enemy shelling did very little damage. Much work returned on those trenches.	
	28.			
	29.			
	30-31.		Relieved in C.1 on night of 29/30 by 9th Black Watch and went into Bde Reserve in old British front line trenches. Working Parties found for work on front system (trenches etc.	

A.J. McAlhorne Lt Colonel

10th Gordons
Vol. 5

D/7078

10th Gordons.

November 1915.

Nov 15

15th Division

K

Army Form C. 2118.

WAR DIARY
or
INTELLIGENCE SUMMARY.
(Erase heading not required.)

10 th (S) Bn Gordon Hghrs

Sheet 1.

November, 1915.

Place	Date	Hour	Summary of Events and Information	Remarks and references to Appendices
Trenches Sector C. 1)	1.		The battalion relieved the 9th BLACK WATCH in front line trenches of Sector C. from G.18.6.68 to The GAP North of HULLUCH ROAD. 47th Division on our right, on our left the 7th CAMERONS. I, K, L companies in the firing line, M company in reserve. Battalion strength 27 officers, 598 other ranks.	
	4.		We were relieved by 9th BLACK WATCH and moved back to reserve trenches in old British support line about G.16.G. 7th CAMERONS on our left, 8th SEAFORTHS, 9th BLACK WATCH in the firing line. The enemy shelled heavily during the relief from 2.30 P.M. to 5 P.M. Sergt McKENZIE of K company was killed. The relief was much impeded by damage done by shells to STONE STREET. All the dug outs in K company's line were blown in.	
Reserve trenches	5.	3.30 A	The Commanding Officer proceeded home on sick leave. A working party of 3 officers and 150 other ranks was sent to WINGS WAY.	
		4 P.M.	A party of 1 officer and 40 men was ordered for work under R.E. on bomb stores, it was followed by 2 similar reliefs at 4 hour intervals	
	7.	6.30 A.M.	The brigade was relieved by the 45 th Brigade and moved back into	

M G Pearson Capt

Army Form C. 2118.

WAR DIARY

or INTELLIGENCE SUMMARY.

Sheet 2.

(Erase heading not required.) 10th (S) Bn GORDON HIGHRS.

November 1915

Place	Date	Hour	Summary of Events and Information	Remarks and references to Appendices
NOEUX.	9.		billets at NOEUX-LES-MINES, arriving about 11:30 a.m. A draft of 1 officer and 50 other ranks arrived. 2nd Lieut F.W. SCOTT was posted to L Company.	
		8 a.m.	O.C. companies left for front trenches in D.R. to survey the ground to be taken over by the battalion.	
		6 a.m.	Working party of 1 officer 25 other ranks on bombing school for 4 hours.	
		9.30 a.m.	Working party of 1 officer 2 sergeants & 78 other ranks as reserve trenches to be taken over by brigade.	
		2.30 a.m.	A relief party to the last party. These two parties were conveyed to VERMELLES in motor buses.	
	10.		Similar working parties as on the 9th.	
	11.			
	12.			
	12.		Battalion strength 28 officers, 737 other ranks.	
NOYELLES.	13.	10.30 a.m.	The 44th brigade relieved the 45th in the trenches. The battalion marched to NOYELLES where they took over billets from 11th R. & S. Highrs. 9th BLACK WATCH, 8th SEAFORTHS in firing line, 7th CAMERONS in local reserve at VERMELLES, GORDONS in local reserve at VERMELLES, GORDONS	

W.G. Pearson Capt

Army Form C. 2118.

WAR DIARY
or
INTELLIGENCE SUMMARY.
(Erase heading not required.)

Sheet 3. 10th (S) BN. GORDON HIGHRS.

November 1915.

Place	Date	Hour	Summary of Events and Information	Remarks and references to Appendices
NOYELLES.			in brigade reserve at NOYELLES. L company billeted at PHILOSOPHE. A permanent working party of 50 other ranks under Lieut HOLLAND billeted at VERMELLES for work under the 73rd R.E. Orders were given to be ready to move off at half an hour's notice during the day, and during the night immediately; all ranks to sleep fully dressed.	
	15.	5 P.M.	2 officers 100 other ranks ⎫	
		5.10 P.M.	2 officers 100 other ranks ⎬ working parties on trench from Pope's Nose to O.B.1.	
		9.30 P.M.	2 officers 150 other ranks ⎭	
			Capt. C.O. GREEN, 7th DRAGOON GUARDS reported for duty, having been posted as 2nd in command to battalion, and took over command.	
Trenches Sector D.2.	16.		The battalion relieved 9th BLACK WATCH in Sector D.2 from G.5.d.4.3 To G.5 B.5U ALLEY (inclusive). 7th CAMERONS on right, 37th brigade 12th Division on left. I, M, K companies in firing line, L in reserve. 9th BLACK WATCH in local reserve at VERMELLES; 8th SEAFORTHS in brigade reserve at NOYELLES.	
	17.	1 P.M.	2nd Lt. G. ROBERTSON and one man killed in centre company in "Hairpin"; Sergt Webster wounded. The enemy shelled our lines between 1 and 3.30 P.M. and did	

M.G. Pearson Capt

Army Form C. 2118.

WAR DIARY
or
INTELLIGENCE SUMMARY.

Sheet 74

(Erase heading not required.)

Army Form C. 2118.

10th (S) Bn. GORDON HIGHRS.

November 1915

Place	Date	Hour	Summary of Events and Information	Remarks and references to Appendices
Trenches Sector D.2	18.		some damage to parapets. The enemy shelled our front, support, and communication trenches.	
VERMELLES	19.		The battalion was relieved by 7th BLACK WATCH and went into local reserve in VERMELLES cellars. 7th CAMERONS in brigade reserve at NOYELLES.	Strength 28 officers 721 other ranks
	20.	9a.m.	Working party 1 officer 50 other ranks on the STANSFIELD ROAD.	
		5 P.M.	Working party 3 officers 150 other ranks on STAFFORD LANE.	
	21.	5 P.M.	Two parties of 1 offr & 20 other ranks clearing up FOSSE WAY daily. Party as at 5 P.M. on 20th.	
Trenches Sector D.2	22.	10.30a.m.	Battalion relieved BLACK WATCH in Sector D.2 as before with some flanking troops. L, I, M companies in firing line, K in support. Capt C. GREEN left to take command of 8th Bn EAST YORKS, 21st division. Enemy put 3 bombs into ESSEX SAP — they were silenced by our own retaliation.	
	23.		Enemy bombed ESSEX SAP, but were completely silenced by bombs, rifle grenades, and trench mortars.	
NOEUX	24.	1.30am	Battalion was relieved by 11th R.S. HIGHRS and went into billets at NOEUX.	
		8.30am	A draft of 74 N.C.O.'s and men arrived.	

N. J. Pearson Capt

Army Form C. 2118.

Sheet 5. **WAR DIARY**
or
INTELLIGENCE SUMMARY. 10th(S) Bn GORDON HIGHRS.
November 1915.
(Erase heading not required.)

Place	Date	Hour	Summary of Events and Information	Remarks and references to Appendices
LABOURSE	26.	9am	Battalion strength 27 officers, 785 other ranks. The battalion marched to billets at LABOURSE. Snow and hard frost.	
	27.	9.30am	Route march by companies by NOEUX-VERQUIN-VERQUIGNEUL-LABOURSE.	
		1.30 p.m.	Parties of 1 officer 10 other ranks per company were instructed in wire entanglements by 74th & 75th R.E. till 4 P.M.	
	28.	11.45 am	Church parade in institute at SALLY LABOURSE.	
		9 a.m.	Working party of 2 officers 100 other ranks in vicinity of VERMELLES. 1 officer 7 men wounded by shell. Officer was 2nd Lieut SPROTT.	
	29.		Companies instructed 3½ hours morning, 1¾ hours afternoon in wire entanglements. A draft of 26 N.C.O.'s and men arrived. Battalion strength 28 officers, 807 other ranks.	
	30.	9 a.m.	Working party of 1 officer 25 other ranks on HULLUCH ROAD trench.	

W.G. Parson Col?
Major Commanding
10th (S) Bn. Gordon Highlanders.

10th Gordons.
Vol. 6

124/7909

10th R Gordons.

December 1915.

13th/Division

CONFIDENTIAL.

War Diary
of
10th (S) Bn Gordon Highrs

From 1st to 31st December 1915.

Army Form C. 2118.

WAR DIARY
INTELLIGENCE SUMMARY.

Title: 10TH (SER) Bn THE GORDON HIGHLANDERS

Month and year: DECEMBER 1915

Place	Date	Hour	Summary of Events and Information	Remarks and references to Appendices
	1		Bn. relieved 13th Bn. Royal Scots in sector C 2. Two platoons of 1/4 Black Watch were on our right, 46th Infantry Brigade on our left. Front extended from point G 5 d. (sheet 36 C.) S.E. the CUPOLA, including THE HAIRPIN. Three Coys in firing line, one in support. Lieut C.G. HARPER and 50 O.R. billeted in NOYELLES as a permanent working party. Enemy shelled sector between 3 P.M. & 6 P.M.	
	2		Enemy bombers opposite ESSEX TRENCH engaged and silenced after 40 mins. Two Germans surrendered to Right Company at night. They reported a wounded German in front. Patrol found and brought him in.	
	3		Capt N.G. PEARSON wounded by a spent bullet in thigh.	
	4		Bn. relieved by 9th BLACK WATCH and moved into support with 14 Cas in OLD BRITISH LINES + 2½ Coys billeted in PHILOSOPHE. Lieut J O PATERSON wounded in shoulder	

WAR DIARY 10TH GORDONS
SHEET 2 INTELLIGENCE SUMMARY. DECEMBER (cont.)

Army Form C. 2118.

Place	Date	Hour	Summary of Events and Information	Remarks and references to Appendices
	5		Capt. W. O.B. Lind heavily shelled about 3 P.M. Casualties :- 3 killed, 3 wounded. Strength 1 Bn. 25 Officers 781 O.R.	
	6.		Bn. relieved 9th BLACK WATCH in C.2.	
	7		Enemy shelled support trenches with H.E. throughout the afternoon with little effect.	
	8		Bombing initiated by us in ESSEX TRENCH continued from 11 A.M. till 4 P.M. One of our bombs destroyed an enemy artificer post. At 10 P.M. enemy shelled ration dump & tramway without effect.	
NOYELLES	10		Bn. relieved by 9th B.W. and moved into Bde. Reserve at NOYELLES. Strength 1 Bn. 25 Officers + 750 O.R.	
	12		2nd Lieut. W. McINTYRE returned for duty.	
	14		Division moved into CORPS RESERVE & 44th BDE. was relieved by 141st I. Bde. 10th GORDONS entrained at NOEUX at 12 NOON and proceeded to LILLERS. Marched from there to	
ALLOUAGNE			ALLOUAGNE. Transport moved by road.	

A.H. Ormsby

WAR DIARY 10TH GORDONS

SHEET 3

Army Form C. 2118.

INTELLIGENCE SUMMARY. DECEMBER (cont.)

Place	Date	Hour	Summary of Events and Information	Remarks and references to Appendices
ALLOUAGNE	15, 16.		Devoted to cleaning up	
	17		Draft 1.470.O.R. under 2nd Lieut. R.A.M. BLACK arrived. Strength of Bn. 27 Officers + 806 O.R.	
	18		Platoon training begun. Snipers and bombers received special instruction under 2nd LIEUT. J.B. WOOD M.C.	
	20.		2nd LIEUT R. RIDDELL reported Col for duty. Lecture to officers by Bde MAJOR on TRENCH DUTIES	
	23		Company training commenced. 2nd Lieuts. R.H. COOPER + J.H. SEMPLE reported for duty. Half Officers + N.C.O.s of Bn. commenced 2-day engineering course.	
	24		Coy training	
	25.		CHRISTMAS DAY. Church parade in morning	
	27		Coy training. Remainder of Officers + N.C.Os commenced 2 day engineering course	
	28		Coy. training	
	29			[signature]

WAR DIARY

10TH GORDONS

INTELLIGENCE SUMMARY. DEC. (con)

SHEET 4

Army Form C. 2118.

Place	Date	Hour	Summary of Events and Information	Remarks and references to Appendices
	30. 31.		2nd LIEUT. C. V. ROBERTS un reported for duty. Coy. training. 2nd Lieut. J. E. LAW rejoined after sick leave. CPL KERR I (ry) awarded D.C.M. for Bravery in Bombing in the HAIRPIN on Dec. 10th Strength 1 Bn. 31 off. 622 o.r.	

H. K. Kaufman Major.
Commdg 10th Bn. GORDON
HIGHLANDERS

[signature]

10½ Giorno
tda: 7

16ᵗ Gadows.
15. Di. E.
Vol. 8

44

January 1916

Diary
of
10th (S) Bn Gordon Highrs

Army Form C. 2118.

10th Batn The Gordon Highlanders

WAR DIARY

INTELLIGENCE SUMMARY

January 1916.

Place	Date	Hour	Summary of Events and Information	Remarks and references to Appendices
ALLOUAGNE	1		The Brigade directed that New Year Day be recognised as a general holiday. The day was devoted to preliminary boxing bouts and football competitions in which the four battalions of the Brigade participated. In the evening a dinner was given to the men of the Battalion in the School. A contribution of twenty pounds was given by the officers, from the Officers' mess fund to defray part of the expenses. The excellent plum puddings were the gift of Sir Duff of Hatton, Aberdeen shire.	
"	2		The morning was given over to Company training. In the afternoon the football matches were continued. Courses:- One Corporal and three men went on a Signalling Course. Two men went on a Trench Mortar Course. Draft:- One officer and twenty other ranks arrived for duty with the Battalion.	

Army Form C. 2118.

WAR DIARY
or
INTELLIGENCE SUMMARY

(Erase heading not required.)

10th Battⁿ The Gordon Highlanders

January (cont.)

Place	Date	Hour	Summary of Events and Information	Remarks and references to Appendices
ALLOUAGNE	2		The Officer was 2nd Lieut. H. L. KNOWLES.	
	3		The day was devoted to Batn Training. - A scheme of attack was carried out. Courses. - 2nd Lieut SEMPLE went to the O.T.S. GOSNAY.	
	4		Batn Training was continued. - Smoke Helmet Drill.	
	5		A Divisional exercise was carried out. The Division trekked to the LILLERS AREA via LIGNY LES AIRES, - AUCHY-AU-BOIS. The 44th Bde Group marched as an Advance Guard to the Division. The Batn spent the night in billets in LIGNY LES AIRES. Courses. - five men went on a Machine Gun Course.	

Army Form C. 2118.

WAR DIARY
or
INTELLIGENCE SUMMARY. 10th Batn The Gordon Highlanders
(Erase heading not required.)

January (cont)

Place	Date	Hour	Summary of Events and Information	Remarks and references to Appendices
ALLOUAGNE	5th		Course (cont). The men went on a Trench Mortar Course.	
	6th		Divisional Exercise (cont). The Trek was continued to COYECQUE and thence back to LIGNY LES AIRES. Where the Batn spent the second night in billets.	
	7.		Divisional Exercise (cont). The Batn marched back to ALLOUAGNE. In this Exercise the 1st Line Transports marched together as a Divisional Transport. The weather conditions during the Trek were comparatively fair, but the roads in places were very heavy.	

1577 Wt.W10791/1773 500,000 1/15 D. D. & L. A.D.S.S./Forms/C. 2118.

WAR DIARY or INTELLIGENCE SUMMARY

10th Batn The Gordon Highlanders

January (cont.)

Army Form C. 2118.

Place	Date	Hour	Summary of Events and Information	Remarks and references to Appendices
ALLOUAGNE	8.		Batn Training was continued. 2nd LIEUT COOPER went on a Trench Mortar Course.	
	9.		The morning was devoted to Batn training. A Gas Demonstration was held at the Bde GRENADIER SCHOOL, Sixteen men from each Batn in the Bde attended. The sixteen included all young Officers who had joined since September last. In the afternoon the final bout of the Boxing Competitions were fought. The Heavy Weight Championship was won by L/Cpl MACKINNON of this Batn. Pte ALLAN, D.C.M. lost the Welter Weight Championship on points after a very evenly contested match. The most interesting contest of the Tournament was the final of the Light-Weights, fought between Sgt O'ROURKE, 7th CAMERONS, and Cpl McLOED 8th SEAFORTHS. Cpl McLOED was awarded the victory after a most interesting match of ten rounds.	

Army Form C. 2118.

WAR DIARY
or
INTELLIGENCE SUMMARY.

10th Batt. The Gordon Highlanders.

Place	Date	Hour	Summary of Events and Information	Remarks and references to Appendices
ALLOUAGNE	9.		General MacCRACKEN, G.O.C. 15th Division was present, also Brig-General WILKINSON, G.O.C. 44th Bde, and Commanding officers of the different units.	
	10.		Battn Training was continued. Courses — 2nd Lieut RIDDELL went to P.O.T.S ROSNAY.	
	11.		Battn Training and refitting was continued. Courses — Three men went on a Trench Mortar Course. The C.O, Company Commanders, Machine Gun Officers and Transport officers left at 7.30 AM on a tour of the 14 BIS SECTOR. The party were taken over from the 1st NORTHAMPTON REGIMENT. The party proceeded by Motor Bus to PHILOSOPHE, and after reporting at HdQrs 5th or 14th BDE recrossed to LOOS battlefield to POSEN STATION. The C.O NORTHANTS conducted the party round the trenches. The party returned by Motor bus	

WAR DIARY

Army Form C. 2118.

10th Battn
The Gordon Highlanders

INTELLIGENCE SUMMARY.

Title page January (contd.)

Place	Date	Hour	Summary of Events and Information	Remarks and references to Appendices
ALLOUAGNE	12		The Battn continued to be refitted with clothing, equipment and necessaries. On this day the Battn provided a working party of 1 Officer and 120 O.R. Sgt MACLAREN L Company was wounded by the accidental explosion of a bomb at the Bde Bombing School. The Battn provided a working party of 1 Officer and 50 O.R. at Bde Bombing school	
	13		The morning was devoted to the cleaning of billets. An inspection of billets was held by the Commanding Officer. The Machine Gun section of the Bde relieved the Machine Guns of the 2nd Bde. A billeting party of 1 NCO and 5 men went to arrange billets for Battn in NOEUX LES MINES.	
	14		The Battn marched to LILLERS from ALLOUAGNE where they entrained for NOEUX LES MINES at 8.45 A.M. Transports were B'requipped and proceeded by road.	

Army Form C. 2118.

10th Batt.
The Gordon Highlanders.

WAR DIARY
or
INTELLIGENCE SUMMARY.
(Erase heading not required.)

Title pages January (1914).

Instructions regarding War Diaries and Intelligence Summaries are contained in F.S. Regs., Part II. and the Staff Manual respectively. Title pages will be prepared in manuscript.

Place	Date	Hour	Summary of Events and Information	Remarks and references to Appendices
MAZINGARBE	14		Dinners were served to the men in NOEUX. Batt. marched from NOEUX by Platoons at one minute interval commencing 3.30 P.M. The Batt. relieved the NORTHAMPTONSHIRE Rgt in 14 BIS SECTION The Relief was completed at 9.30 P.M. During the relief 5 men of the 8th SEAFORTHS were killed by a shell.	
	15.		One Platoon of the ROYAL IRISH Rgt was attached to each Company for instruction. In the evening J Co. took over from a Company of the 9th BLACK WATCH on the left. The line from VENDIN ALLEY (incl.) to BROADWAY. J Co. Reld from VENDIN ALLEY to BOYAU at H.19.C.6.7½. M Co handed over to SEAFORTHS line from H.25.A.5.2 to POSEN ALLEY, and took over from J Co. up to BOYAU at H.19.C.6.7½. M Co occupied frontage from BOYAU A.19.C.6.7½.(excl.) to POSEN ALLEY (incl.). Draft. Draft of 60 (sixty) other ranks reported for duty with the Batt.	

WAR DIARY
or
INTELLIGENCE SUMMARY.

Army Form C. 2118.

10th Battn. 103rd Gordon Highlanders

Month: January (contd.)

Place	Date	Hour	Summary of Events and Information	Remarks and references to Appendices
MAZINGARBE	15		In the afternoon our Artillery bombarded the enemy trenches between two and three o'clock. Situation - Normal. Casualties - Nil.	
	16		Sgt BISHOP proceeded by 11 A.M. train from BETHUNE to ROUEN on duty in connection with records. One Officer and 25 O.R. were sent down to be billeted in PHILOSOPHE to take over Control Post, Bath House etc from ROYAL IRISH. Progress Report - Enemy Sniper at H.19.a.7.2.5 was silenced by our snipers. Trench boards lifted and cleaned in Fire Trench. POSEN ALLEY cleared from Support Trench to Fire Trench, and traverses in Reserve Trench revetted.	
		4 a.m.	A loud buzzing noise such as might be made by a large fly-wheel was heard in Fire Trench, between 12 midnight and 3 A.M.	

WAR DIARY
INTELLIGENCE SUMMARY

Army Form C. 2118.

10th Batn The Gordon Highlanders

Place	Date	Hour	Summary of Events and Information	Remarks and references to Appendices
MAZINGARBE	16		We were unable to locate the man. Two Officers of the 9th Batn carried out a Reconnaissance in front of our line at night.	
	17		Courses:- Four men proceeded on Machine Gun Courses at GOSNAY. Two on a VICKERS Course, two on a LEWIS Course. The 9th BLACK WATCH relieved us in the front line. The relief was completed at 10.30 p.m. Progress Report:- A Machine Gun sprayed our parapet in H.19.A. but was eventually silenced by one of our guns. Snipers were fairly active against our trenches in H.19.C. Our snipers being on claim to have shot at least one German opposite H.19.E. Patrol went out at 7 P.M from top of VENDIN ALLEY, N.E worked towards Cross roads and ruined estaminet at H.19.A.6.6 where new trench was recently reported to be under construction.	

WAR DIARY
INTELLIGENCE SUMMARY

Army Form C. 2118.

10th Batn. The Gordon Highlanders

January (cont'd).

Place	Date	Hour	Summary of Events and Information	Remarks and references to Appendices
MAZINGARBE	17.		Owing to moonlight thy could not get very close, but work was undoubted in progress; it is thought that a drill was being used. Between 3 AM and 4.7 rounds of heating bandages and cheering in stakes could be heard from enemy trenches opposite. A party of 100 worked at new Support Trench, working North from POSEN ALLEY.	
	18.		Working Parties. A party of 1 officer and 50.O.R. reported to 9th Black Watch at 6 P.M. A party of 1 officer and 50.O.R. Progress Report. Trench between C.23.c.3.9 and C.23.a.5.2. L£ shelled shelled between 10 A.M. and 10.30 A.M. Battn relieved 9th Black Watch in TENTH AVENUE and Keeps.	
	19.		Machine Gun Officer was relieved by the Reserve Officer.	

Army Form C. 2118.

10th Batn
The Gordon Highlanders

WAR DIARY
or
INTELLIGENCE SUMMARY.
(Erase heading not required.)

Instructions regarding War Diaries and Intelligence Summaries are contained in F. S. Regs., Part II. and the Staff Manual respectively. Title pages will be prepared in manuscript.

Place	Date	Hour	Summary of Events and Information	Remarks and references to Appendices
MAZINGARBE	19.		Progress Report - Enemy shelled Reserve Trenches in TENTH AVENUE intermittently during the day; also PONT STREET. No damage was done here, but considerable damage was done in LENS ROAD REDOUBT by bombardment. 8th SEAFORTHS reported enemy mining in vicinity of firing line about H.25.C.22. A permanent listening post was established.	
	20		A working party was detailed to work on RAILWAY ALLEY near GUN ALLEY. Batn relieved the 8th SEAFORTHS. Relief was reported complete 11.40 p.m. Further parties worked in VENDIN ALLEY, QUEENSWAY, RESERVE TRENCH &c. LENS ROAD REDOUBT shelled about 11 AM. One man accidentally killed while cleaning his rifle. Casualty Report.	
	21		Enemy were working during the night on their second line on PUITS 14 BIS	

1577 Wt.W10791/1773 500,000 1/15 D.D.&L. A.D.S.S./Forms/C. 2118.

Army Form C. 2118.

Instructions regarding War Diaries and Intelligence
Summaries are contained in F. S. Regs., Part II.
and the Staff Manual respectively. Title pages
will be prepared in manuscript.

WAR DIARY
or
INTELLIGENCE SUMMARY.
(Erase heading not required.)

10th Battn
The Gordon Highlanders

Place	Date	Hour	Summary of Events and Information	Remarks and references to Appendices
MAZINGARBE	21		At 10 A.M. the Right Coy's trenches at H31 d.09 were enfiladed from right flank by various projectiles which burst about our trench. Patrol went over enemy lines at H25.c.6.9, and found it very poor. German trenches there seemed unoccupied. Casualties O.R. One wounded.	
	22		Enemy shelled Loos fairly heavily about 3.30 P.M. Patrol went out at 6.30 P.M. one went up W side of LENS - CITE - ST ELIE road towards PUITS 14 BIS. Trench running along W side of road was shallow and not continuous. Casualties - nil.	
	23		Enemy sprayed our parapets with Machine Guns in the mist this morning. Loos was fairly heavily shelled for ½ hr. about 3.30 P.M. An officers patrol went out in the evening, they reached H25.c.74, and found the enemy wire very strong and in thick loose entanglements	

Army Form C. 2118.

WAR DIARY
or
INTELLIGENCE SUMMARY.

10th Batn
Gordon Highlanders

January (cont.)

(Erase heading not required.)

Instructions regarding War Diaries and Intelligence Summaries are contained in F. S. Regs., Part II. and the Staff Manual respectively. Title pages will be prepared in manuscript.

Place	Date	Hour	Summary of Events and Information	Remarks and references to Appendices
MAZINGARBE	23		Draft. Draft of 7 Officers O.R. arrived for duty with the Battn. They remained in huts in HAZINGARBE. Casualties. 1 man wounded, 1 wounded and duty.	
	24		Party of 8th K.O.S.B. Officers joined our trenches. The enemy artillery was active throughout the morning. Parties worked in CHALK PIT ALLEY, SUFFOLK Trench and POSEN ALLEY. Casualties. Two men wounded and duty.	
	25		LIEUT. J.G. PATERSON rejoined for duty with the Battn. Battn positions relieved by 8th K.O.S.B. Casualties. One man wounded.	
	26		Battn was relieved by 8th K.O.S.B. Loos heavily shelled between 1.10 P.m and 2.45 P.m Enemy artillery much more active than usual	

Army Form C. 2118.

WAR DIARY
or
INTELLIGENCE SUMMARY.
(Erase heading not required.)

Instructions regarding War Diaries and Intelligence Summaries are contained in F. S. Regs., Part II. and the Staff Manual respectively. Title pages will be prepared in manuscript.

Place	Date	Hour	Summary of Events and Information	Remarks and references to Appendices
MAZINGARBE	26		Casualties. Three men wounded. This happened during the relief.	
	27		LIEUT E. W. HANCOCK was wounded at ENGLAND with Enemy artillery again very active. Loos was again heavily shelled.	
	28		Major W. W. MACGREGOR. D.S.O. reported his arrival for duty with this Battn, and assumes Temporary Command (Auth A.G. 7/9s 33 a 17/1/16	
	29.		Major H. K. LONGMAN went to take over Command of O.T.S GOSNAY	
	30		Battn resting and refitting in MAZINGARBE.	
	31		Several shells were dropped in the vicinity of the Church, MAZINGARBE.	

Army Form C. 2118.

WAR DIARY
or
INTELLIGENCE SUMMARY.
(Erase heading not required.)

10th Battn. The Gordon Highlanders.

Title pages January

Place	Date	Hour	Summary of Events and Information	Remarks and references to Appendices
MAZINGARBE			Strength of Battn 1/1/16:—	
			Officers 32.	
			O.R. 823.	
			31/1/16. Officers 34.	
			O.R. 866.	
			To hospital — sick :—	
			Officers. 3.	
			O.R. 56. (of which 39 returned)	
			Wounded :—	
			Officers — nil	
			O.R. — 16 (of which 2 returned).	
			J. B. McKenzie Lt.	
			10th Gordon Hrs.	

CONFIDENTIAL.

From
> Officer Commanding
> > 10th(S)Bn Gordon Highlrs.

To, *Officer i/c*
~~The~~ D.A.G. *Office*
~~3rd Echelon~~
> > > Base.

Herewith original War Diary of this Battalion for the month of February 1916.

J.E. Husband
2nd Lieut. for Captain & A/Adjutant
10th(S)Bn Gordon Highlrs.

5th March 1916.

Army Form C. 2118.

WAR DIARY
or
INTELLIGENCE SUMMARY.
(Erase heading not required.)

Instructions regarding War Diaries and Intelligence Summaries are contained in F. S. Regs., Part II. and the Staff Manual respectively. Title pages will be prepared in manuscript.

Place	Date	Hour	Summary of Events and Information	Remarks and references to Appendices
	19.6			
MAZINGARBE to Trenches.	Feb. 1.		The 44th Brigade completed their 6 days rest in Divisional Reserve stock over the HULLUCH Section of trenches today. This extends from DEVON LANE — Square C12d to VENDIN ALLEY — Square H19a. The 10th Gordon Highlanders were in Brigade support & leaving MAZINGARBE about 4 p.m. with platoons at 7 minute intervals had relieved the 6th Cameron Highlanders resting down by about 8 p.m. The trenches occupied were Bn. H.Qrs. in 9th Avenue — the Bn. in 10th Avenue & O.B. 2 & 3. Two days rations were carried up — than is not a good plan but it was done to keep the transport as much as possible off the HULLUCH Road, which is sometimes shelled & makes nice machine gun. The night was very dark but much work was done, to give the new line to settle down. Working parties found men — 1 N.C.O. & 10 men Sappy 6 horses to arrival to 253rd Tunnelling Coy. R.E. to carry away chalk from mining shafts. The firing line packs were not taken up to the trenches but stored into the blankets & the men were much better without them. 14 men sent to Hospital.	Reference to Trench Map 36 c N.W. 3 Edition 6 Scale 1:10000

Army Form C. 2118.

WAR DIARY
or
INTELLIGENCE SUMMARY.
(Erase heading not required.)

Instructions regarding War Diaries and Intelligence Summaries are contained in F. S. Regs., Part II. and the Staff Manual respectively. Title pages will be prepared in manuscript.

Place	Date	Hour	Summary of Events and Information	Remarks and references to Appendices
	1916			
TRENCHES	Feb 2		A fine & quiet day.	
			At night 300 men of the Battalion were working on communication trenches HAY ALLEY & ESSEX LANE, throwing back the parapet about 1 foot. The 73rd Co. R.E. under whom they were working were very pleased with the work.	
			The 1 N.C.O. & 10 men busy 6 hours still continued under the 253rd Co. R.E. The wind was more or less fully watched as it was thought the Germans might make a gas attack if it was in the E. Today it was S.W. the General said it would probably be N.E. tomorrow.	
			1 man very slightly wounded, eye bruised from bit of shrapnel falling from shell bursting overhead. 5 men sent down sick. 2nd Lt. P.W. SCOTT to hospital.	
do	" 3		A fine quiet day. Wind S. changing to W.	
			At night 300 men working on HAY ALLEY & ESSEX LANE deepening & repairing. The 1 N.C.O. & 10 men busy 6 hours still continued under the 253rd Co. R.E. & carrying party of 30 men for the 253rd Co. R.E. sent to the trench VERMELLES & had a fruitless journey, as no one was there to meet them.	
			3 men very slightly wounded, eyes from dreadful heat of aeroplane. 9 men sent down sick.	

Army Form C. 2118.

WAR DIARY
or
INTELLIGENCE SUMMARY.
(Erase heading not required.)

Instructions regarding War Diaries and Intelligence Summaries are contained in F.S. Regs., Part II. and the Staff Manual respectively. Title pages will be prepared in manuscript.

Place	Date	Hour	Summary of Events and Information	Remarks and references to Appendices
TRENCHES	1916 Feb 4		A fine quiet day. Wind S. partially S.E. for a time veering to S.W. Relieved half 7th Cameron Highlanders in the front line taking over the left sub section which extends from DEVON LANE in Square G12d to SIXTH AVENUE (exclusive) in Square Brick H13a. The relief was carried out without trouble in the evening. On our right were the 9th Black Watch, on our left dismounted cavalry. The firing line was occupied by M. & L. Coys. K in support, I in reserve. The line is a very long one about 1300 yards. The Germans have been very active in mining operations. Have already exploded two mines known to have strength nearly to left of M. & 353 in G. R.E. are counter mining, but the enemy have the good a start — so the line where it is known is very lightly held. Listeners are attached. 8 machine guns are allotted to the front line & 2 from a Motor M.G. Battery to the Reserve line. 2 Batteries 72nd Brigade R.F.A. support the line. "C" Battery firing over the right company "D" Battery over the left.	

T.134. Wt. W.708—776. 500000. 4/15. Sir J. C. & S.

Army Form C. 2118.

WAR DIARY
or
INTELLIGENCE SUMMARY.
(Erase heading not required.)

Instructions regarding War Diaries and Intelligence Summaries are contained in F. S. Regs., Part II. and the Staff Manual respectively. Title pages will be prepared in manuscript.

Place	Date 1916	Hour	Summary of Events and Information	Remarks and references to Appendices
TRENCHES	4 Feb		**Neuve Chapelle.** Two days rations were sent up after dark & there was rather a muddle about it – with the raids made it takes 12 carts to bring & them up in consequence a large carrying party.	
—do—	5 "		A quiet afternoon, wind S.W. changing to W. Last night a patrol from C Coy went out under 2⁰ Lieut. R.M. RIDDEL having no trouble by CARDIFF SAP. Then they dug? then to examine some of the many numerous sap heads that the enemy are throwing out along the whole of their front. These sap heads may be for many gas or liquid fire, or simply to be converted into a new front line. The patrol found the sap about 40 yards away & at present no signs of arrangements for a gas or flame attack. M. Coy also sent out 2 patrols under The ground around BREGON SAP & the nine craters were examined – the enemy sniping was very active. Enemy Snipers all night & a number of rifle Grenades were thrown into our trench, but no damage was done, & our trenches although (see next page)	

Army Form C. 2118.

WAR DIARY
or
INTELLIGENCE SUMMARY.
(Erase heading not required.)

Instructions regarding War Diaries and Intelligence Summaries are contained in F. S. Regs., Part II. and the Staff Manual respectively. Title pages will be prepared in manuscript.

Place	Date	Hour	Summary of Events and Information	Remarks and references to Appendices
	1916			
TRENCHES	5 Feb.		1 man was killed by a rifle grenade, 2 were wounded, 1 very slightly wounded.	
— do —			3 men sent down sick.	
		5 p.m.	The head of CARDIFF SAP was bombarded with H.E. 4.2" shells & about 30 rifle grenades were fired over.	
		6.20 pm	Bombardment repeated — were bombardments were probably in retaliation for our	
			— do — } activity with rifle grenades.	
		9.0 pm	In each case our field artillery retaliated, at our request on enemy front line.	
— do —	6 Feb.		Normal day. Wind S. changing to S.W. or W.S.W.	
		4.0 am	Enemy exploded a mine on our left opposite to line held by the dismounted cavalry, but they were too previous. It did no damage.	
			At night a patrol of D Coy under 2nd Lieut. R.M RIDDEL was out- from CARDIFF SAP & again inspected enemy saps which they found unoccupied — but enemy were heard working in their front line.	
			Two patrols went out from M Coy under —	
			1 went from NEWPORT SAP — also reconnoitred an enemy sap which they found unoccupied, they bombed the mine crater near MERTHYR SAP, enemy retaliated with rifle grenades.	

WAR DIARY
or
INTELLIGENCE SUMMARY.
(Erase heading not required.)

Army Form C. 2118.

Instructions regarding War Diaries and Intelligence Summaries are contained in F. S. Regs., Part II. and the Staff Manual respectively. Title pages will be prepared in manuscript.

Place	Date	Hour	Summary of Events and Information	Remarks and references to Appendices
TRENCHES	1916 6/7/16		Work was also carried out on the Support line making fire steps & clearing & repairing literal boards. M.G. on the left also completed 48 yards running. 1 G. on the right also repaired a disappeared line. Rifle grenades were intermittently thrown into enemy trenches & at night machine gun occasionally swept enemy parapet. 3 men wounded (slightly), sent down sick. Normal day. Wind S.W. to W. Officers patrols were again out at night — information which the same as before. A start was made into connected main shallow between traverses of parados, chiefly for protection against "Rauenwerfer". 50 men under 13th G.R.E. worked on fire steps in the support line. Party was sent to MAZINGARBE for rifle grenades. At night enemy was again continued by both companies. Enemy machine guns traversed our trenches at all times during tonight.	
—do—	7	1-1.30 a.m.	Front support line shelled by 4.2"	

Army Form C. 2118.

WAR DIARY
or
INTELLIGENCE SUMMARY.
(Erase heading not required.)

Place	Date	Hour	Summary of Events and Information	Remarks and references to Appendices
TRENCHES	7 Feb. 1916		1 man sent down sick.	
do	8am	11. am	A number of rifle grenades fired into our trench. Our retaliation & assisted by the 19th T.M. Battery completely silenced enemy.	
		4. pm	Our snipers were active. Enemy seemed to take a great interest in their signalled results of shots into shovels.	
PHILOSOPHE			Enemy working party in a communication trench was fired on by our field artillery, the artillery observation officers could not see the place & the observation was done by Captains THOM & MOFFAT who by times shortening the range 25 yards were successful in getting some shells right into the enemy trench.	
			At night work was again carried on in fire stepping support trench - wiring was done on front support line.	
			The Battalion were relieved at night by the 7th Cameron Highlanders & moved into billets in PHILOSOPHE where they went in. Ruryard Avenue. The relief was carried out successfully & got the Battalion put in between 9.30 p.m. & 10.30 p.m. When a working party of 7 officers & 230 men were found by day to clear up RUTOIRE ALLEY — duration of work 6 hours.	

T.1134. Wt. W708—776. 500000. 4/15. Sir J. C. & S.

Army Form C. 2118.

WAR DIARY
or
INTELLIGENCE SUMMARY.
(Erase heading not required.)

Place	Date	Hour	Summary of Events and Information	Remarks and references to Appendices
PHILOSOPHE	1916 7 Feb.		Immediately on arrival a working party of 1 Officer & 60 men were found for finishing material up railway to R.E. dump.	
		5.30 pm	16 men reported at Zone 3 for work under R.E.	
		5.30 pm	A control post 1 N.C.O. + 2 men found at CHAPEL KEEP to regulate transport. A Brigade guard was found 1 Sergt. 3 Corpls. 16 men to remain on duty 3 days.	
do — 8 -			Working parties were found as under —	
		8.00 am	25 men at Zone 3 working under R.E.	
			1 Officer 20 men working on RUTOIRE ALLEY for 6 hours.	
		5.0 pm	2 N.C.O.s & 12 men Brigade Grenade Store PHILOSOPHE.	
		5.0 pm	1 N.C.O. 2 men control post CHAPEL KEEP.	
		4.0 pm	3 & 4 Officers 150 men for work in reserve trench between HAY ALLEY & HOLLY LANE this party returned 11.30 p.m.	
		9.30 pm	1 Officer 60 men for work under R.E. pushing up stores.	
			1 N.C.o. & 3 men on Brigade fatigue.	

WAR DIARY
or
INTELLIGENCE SUMMARY.
(Erase heading not required.)

Army Form C. 2118.

Place	Date	Hour	Summary of Events and Information	Remarks and references to Appendices
PHILOSOPHE	1916 8 Feb.		No. 15201 Pte. J. W. Green "I" Coy. had an adventure one time; he was away on a working party, when a shell burst near him, a bit straining his foot & slightly wounding it — he lifted up a shovel he had in his hand with a jerk & cut his ear. No sooner had he done that than another shell came & a brick hit him in the middle of his back — but his nerve he repairs simply wants a few days rest. He was sent to hospital.	
— do —	9 —		Gas alarm practice in the morning. Pte. G. C. HOLLAND sent to hospital sick. also 6 men. The following working parties were found — 4 offrs. 200 men constructing fire steps, repairing parapet or on reserve trench between HOLLY LANE & HAY ALLEY — left 4 p.m. returned 11.30 p.m. 1 off. 10 men clearing trench gratings & sump pits in RUTOIRE ALLEY. 9 men unloading stones filling up at VICTORIA STATION. 1 off. 30 men carrying up & laying slag on railway track. 13 men loading wagons at Farm 3. 30 men taking stones from Farm 3 to POSEN STATION. 1 N.C.O. & 10 men working at Ruingate Running Stores. 1 man wounded on working party at night.	

Army Form C. 2118.

WAR DIARY
or
INTELLIGENCE SUMMARY.
(Erase heading not required.)

Instructions regarding War Diaries and Intelligence Summaries are contained in F. S. Regs., Part II. and the Staff Manual respectively. Title pages will be prepared in manuscript.

Place	Date 1916	Hour	Summary of Events and Information	Remarks and references to Appendices
PHILOSOPHE & TRENCHES	10.7.16.	4.	3rd Battalion drawn in reserve for Lieuten. Battalion relieved 7th Cameron Highlanders in the left sub-section of the HULLUCH section of trenches, holding the firing line, support & reserve trenches in the same place as before. No position of the companies was changed.	
		4.15pm	The leading platoon passed the cross roads at PHILOSOPHE & the relief was reported complete about 7.30pm. Two days rations were carried up by the men. A very quiet night indeed. 2Lt RIDDEL & Pte McARTHUR of L Coy. were out on patrol & reconnoitred enemy saps, but found no work in progress. An officers patrol was also sent out by M Coy. Work at night was carried on in the Support Trench by "K" Coy. "L" Coy. was responsible for carrying up water. Working parties were found to assist the 253rd Tunnelling Coy. R.E. in emptying sandbags excavated from their shafts. The usual work in repairing trenches carried on. 2Lt W. McINTYRE was sent to hospital sick — also 8 men. 1 man wounded — 1 man accidentally wounded at Brigade Bombing School.	

T/134. Wt. W708—776. 500000. 4/15. Sir J. C. & S.

Army Form C. 2118.

WAR DIARY
or
INTELLIGENCE SUMMARY.
(Erase heading not required.)

Instructions regarding War Diaries and Intelligence Summaries are contained in F. S. Regs., Part II. and the Staff Manual respectively. Title pages will be prepared in manuscript.

Place	Date	Hour	Summary of Events and Information	Remarks and references to Appendices
TRENCHES	1916 11 Feb.		Unpleasant day, drizzling all day. Wind S.E. A wind that might be favourable for a German gas attack, so a message came from the Division ordering the "Gas Alert" but no gas came & the alert was cancelled in the evening when the wind changed. A quiet morning, but a busy afternoon. The Germans exploded a small mine in our trenches, which was, as usual, accompanied by heavy shelling by artillery on both sides.	
		1.30 pm	Their own support line from STONE STREET to DEVON LANE was bombarded with rifle grenades.	
		3.30 pm	Our own support line was bombarded with heavy shells, which mostly fell in a part that was unoccupied.	
		4.45 pm	Several trench mortar bombs were thrown into our trenches in the night.	
		5.0 pm	The bombardment became intense, every sort of shell being fired at our trenches.	
		5.20 pm	Mine was exploded & the Germans immediately opened heavy rifle & machine gun fire, but our men & guns were too much for them & the German bullets were soon ceased coming, our men having entirely the upper hand.	
		6.0 pm	Everything quiet.	

Army Form C. 2118.

WAR DIARY
or
INTELLIGENCE SUMMARY.
(Erase heading not required.)

Place	Date	Hour	Summary of Events and Information	Remarks and references to Appendices
TRENCHES	11.2.16		The position where the mine was exploded was just N. of Sixth Avenue about the junction from line H 13 a 11. The size of the crater formed about 15' across x 10' full; its sending in our fire trench so that the outer lip could be reached into a fire parapet. It was soon lined & killed by the explosion & three bodies were never recovered. 2 men were badly shaken. The Germans made no attempt to advance. M Coy. sent out a patrol (2nd Lt BLACK & Corpl TOWERS) & found everything very quiet & very little enemy spring on in every line. L Coy sent out a patrol (L/Cpl GILMORE, Pte CONDIE) which reconnoitred some of the enemy sapps & found no much spring on. In addition to mine commotion Sergt MARSHALL was hit in the eye by a bullet but not killed - his N.C.O. used not have come up to the trenches, as he had a sprained ankle, but he insisted on staying to duty. 1 man was hit by a rifle grenade that did not explode - but it knocked him down rather badly.	
-do-		Tues 9	Black Watch who were on our right took over the large of the fire trenches about 200 yards on our Battalion front was relieving. Took place at 11pm. our night. 3 men sent to hospital.	

T/2134. Wt. W708—776. 500000. 4/15. Sir J.C. & B.

WAR DIARY or INTELLIGENCE SUMMARY

Army Form C. 2118.

Place	Date	Hour	Summary of Events and Information	Remarks and references to Appendices
TRENCHES	1916 12th		A fairly quiet day so far as we were concerned, but enemy artillery very active on both sides of us. Wind N.b.N.W. Fine day. At night ("midnight") a mine was exploded by our Engineers on our left, but to our astonishment no infantry action followed. Great dissatisfaction & disappointment among the men as pea soup dinners were substituted for the usual warm ration. The main ration is served soon after daylight & anger when the men up after a night on the fire step & the substitution of pea soup was looked on as a great hardship.	
		2-4pm	Some shelling of our front line trench. Very heavy shelling was going on our right & left, but our line was very fairly quiet. Officers patrols were out at night from both companies. Enemy were working in their front line trench & artillery fire was opened on them & work stopped. Work was again done on the Suffolk Trench & DEVON LANE Chaus up. 1 man very slightly wounded still at duty - none sent to Hospital.	

Army Form C. 2118.

WAR DIARY
or
INTELLIGENCE SUMMARY.
(Erase heading not required.)

Instructions regarding War Diaries and Intelligence Summaries are contained in F. S. Regs., Part II. and the Staff Manual respectively. Title pages will be prepared in manuscript.

Place	Date	Hour	Summary of Events and Information	Remarks and references to Appendices
Copy from Sketch	13/2/1916		SKETCH showing MINES and COUNTER MINES in left sub-section HULLUCH SECTION. Position on Map 36c N.W.3. Edition 6. Square G.14 & 28 — G.2 & 75	

DEVON LANE

FIRE TRENCH

NEWPORT SAP

CRATERS

BRECON SAP

MERTHYR SAP

SUPPORT TRENCH

⊙ Our Shafts working & listening
● A.D.E.F. Enemy Mines charged & tamped
▢ T Loophole Traverses.

——— Fire Trench.
∙∙∙∙∙ No Support Trench — not firestepped
- - - - Projected Fire Trench

T/134. Wt. W708—776. 500000. 4/15. Sr J. C. & S.

WAR DIARY
or
INTELLIGENCE SUMMARY.
(Erase heading not required.)

Army Form C. 2118.

Place	Date	Hour	Summary of Events and Information	Remarks and references to Appendices
	1916			
TRENCHES	13 Feb.		The 46th Infantry Brigade relieved the 44th Brigade in the HULLUCH Section. The latter Brigade went into Divisional Reserve.	
to			A quiet day. Atmosphere. Wind W. Zero. The Battalion was relieved by the 7th K.O.S.B.'s. The relieving Battalion left France the cross roads at PHILOSOPHE at 10.30 am. The relief was completed by 2.10 pm. & the Battalion were clear of the trenches by 3.15 pm. Marched straight on to billets at	
NOEUX LES MINES			The relief went very smoothly. There was no shelling on our part of the line, although it was very heavy on our left. 3 men sent to Hospital.	
			A Church of England padre is attached to the Battalion — DeVINE — if ever wanted, he is to be found in the firing line distributing Woodbine cigarettes.	

Army Form C. 2118.

WAR DIARY
or
INTELLIGENCE SUMMARY.
(Erase heading not required.)

Instructions regarding War Diaries and Intelligence Summaries are contained in F. S. Regs., Part II. and the Staff Manual respectively. Title pages will be prepared in manuscript.

Place	Date	Hour	Summary of Events and Information	Remarks and references to Appendices
	1916			
NOEUX LES MINES	16 Feb.		The total casualties for the last tour in the trenches from 1st to 13th Feb. have been:—	
			Sent to Hospital — 3 Officers 60 other ranks.	
			Strength	
			Killed 5 — 31 Officers	
			Wounded 18 — 817 other ranks	
			3 — 83 848	
			Numbers returned —	
			From Hospital 10	
			Wounded 3	
			Total wastage 3 — 70.	
			Although the strength shown 31 Officers 100 are away sick or on other jobs.	
			Major A. K. Dempsey — O 15th Aust. Officers training school.	
			Capt. A. P. Pattull — do —	
			Lieut. A. Inglis — Attd. Bde. Bombing School.	
			away { Lt-Col. Wallace	
			{ W. E. W. Hancock	
			{ " G. C. Holland	
			sick { 2" " C. V. Robertson	
			{ " P. W. Scott	
			{ " W. Int. Inglis	
			Lieut. F. W. Gordon	

WAR DIARY or INTELLIGENCE SUMMARY.

Army Form C. 2118.

Place	Date	Hour	Summary of Events and Information	Remarks and references to Appendices
	1916			
NOEUX LES MINES	Feb 14		Working parties, while in billets are to be found daily for work under the Town Major. 1 NCO 12 men at 8.30 am to 2 pm. Total 2 N.C.O.s 24 men.	
- do -	15		Very high W. wind in morning followed by rain. The Rates were allotted to the Battalion. 2/Lt. A.F. SPROTT rejoins the Battalion, having been wounded on 29 Nov 1915. Men out on a working party.	
- do -	16		Nothing to record	
- do -	17		A working party 1 Officer 85 other ranks was found for work under 216 Co. R.E. The C.O. inspected equipment & rifles of the Battalion, noted the exception of "J" "I" Coy. Great improvement in it. None is necessary.	
- do -	18		Working parties found as of under — 2 Officers 100 men Farm 3 PHILOSOPHE at 9.30 am 2 " 100 " Church MAZINGARBE at 8.30 am 6 " 300 " X Roads PHILOSOPHE at 5.30 pm.	

Army Form C. 2118.

WAR DIARY
or
INTELLIGENCE SUMMARY.
(Erase heading not required.)

Instructions regarding War Diaries and Intelligence Summaries are contained in F. S. Regs., Part II. and the Staff Manual respectively. Title pages will be prepared in manuscript.

Place	Date 1916	Hour	Summary of Events and Information	Remarks and references to Appendices
NOEUX LES MINES	18 Feb.		Extract from 4th Corps routine orders — 839. Appreciation of Services — The names of the following officers N.C.O's have been brought to notice by G.H.Q. as having rendered especially good services in the training of reinforcements during Dec. 1915 & January 1916 — Staples - 15th Division - Captain F.J.C. MOFFAT - 10th Gordon Highlanders. It was decided to mark the event & work up the Pipe Band & a number of men never left out of the trenches hitherto.	
NOEUX LES MINES to TRENCHES	19 Feb.		The 44th Infantry Brigade relieves the 46th Infantry Brigade in the PUITS 14 BIS Section. The 10th Gordon Highlanders were in Brigade Support for the first 3 days, but will be in the firing for the next nine. The starting point at NOEUX LES MINES was passed by the 1st Company at 12.30 p.m. the rest taken was via MAZINGARBE & PHILOSOPHE, where the communication trench NORTHERN UP was entered. The relief went very smoothly & the 7th Royal Scots Fusiliers were relieved by 4 p.m. The Battalion was in Support, have crossed 2 platoons of "I" Coy in 65 metre front network & 2 platoons "I" Coy Northern Sap Redoubt, "L" Coy & "M" Coy in 10th Avenue.	

T2134. W! W798-776. 500000. 4/15. Sir J. C. & S.

WAR DIARY
or
INTELLIGENCE SUMMARY.
(Erase heading not required.)

Army Form C. 2118.

Place	Date	Hour	Summary of Events and Information	Remarks and references to Appendices
TRENCHES	1916 19 Feb.		These 3 companies are all in 10th Avenue, but the frontage extends for 2100 yards. "K" Coy. in GUN ALLEY, about 200 yards (by tunnel) from Battalion Headquarters in PONT STREET. The trenches are mostly boarded & clean, but-parts if very wet-Tuesday. The Headquarters dug out, must have been an old German one, as it is papered & has wooden beds & two fireplaces, very interior of sea scapes — not so safe as at night be, but for that reason, more comfortable, as long as too many shells don't come down. Rations are taken by the transport to VICTORIA STATION then further up the tramway to POSEN STATION — which is quite close, to the rationing & work has rarely been much. Men are some water tanks, which are filled by a pump at PHILOSOPHE 2 miles away that helps with the water supply. Being a relief night several work was done, but a stout man made is clearing up 10th Avenue. The other Battalion of the Brigade relieves the front-line by night.	

WAR DIARY or INTELLIGENCE SUMMARY

Army Form C. 2118.

Place	Date 1916	Hour	Summary of Events and Information	Remarks and references to Appendices
TRENCHES	19 Feb.		The wind most annoyingly changed to the E. stolen from "Gas alert" came at 12 noon. This means extra sentries to make up men who may be sleeping by day, put an infestation of gas helmets twice daily & general alertness. In the evening the Germans did make a gas attack near GIVENCHY - S. of LENS. Otherwise an uneventful day - 5 H.E. shrapnel were fired at 10 Avenue but did no damage. 2 were duds. No. 78460 Sergeant W. MASSON, No. 14358 Sergeant J. KERR went into NOEUX LES MINES & were congratulated by General Sir Chas Monro K.C.B. commanding 1st Army on having been awarded the D.C.M.	
— do —	20 Feb.		Weather nearly too whole Battalion were on working parties – laying treads in 10th Avenue & PONT Street clearing up & deepening LOOS & ENGLISH ALLEYS. Wind still in the EAST. Heavy firing in his afternoon from where side of LOOS probably Germans.	
— do —	21 Feb.		Extract from 15th Division Summary of Operations dated 18th February – "the 4th H.V. Gun (known as COTTER) was fired on about 3.15 p.m. Instead rounds off having done little to improve his average." MAZINGARBE. Its length has however severate and he was soon taken	

Army Form C. 2118.

WAR DIARY
or
INTELLIGENCE SUMMARY.
(Erase heading not required.)

Place	Date	Hour	Summary of Events and Information	Remarks and references to Appendices
TRENCHES	1916 21 Feb.		Work consisted of cleaning up trenches & laying down trench boards. Working parties almost tied trench boards in ENGLISH ALLEY for about 200 yds. Support trench from ENGLISH ALLEY for 200 yds. S. was deepened & widened. Cleaning up to AVENUE & GUN TRENCH. 10 men working under the R.E. in RAILWAY ALLEY. Wind changed to W. & "Gas alert" was cancelled.	
- do -	22 Feb.		Fine early, followed by snow. By W.O. letter of today's date Lieut: Colonel H.R. WALLACE was struck off the strength of the Battalion; not having been passed fit by a medical board.	

WAR DIARY
or
INTELLIGENCE SUMMARY.
(Erase heading not required.)

Place	Date	Hour	Summary of Events and Information	Remarks and references to Appendices
TRENCHES	1916 22 Feb.		The Battalion relieved the 9th Black Watch in the centre sub section of the Bde PUITS 14 bis. The relief commenced from 10.0 & was at 5.30 p.m. reported complete at 8.11 p.m. A very quiet & satisfactory relief. Weather fine, the enemy having cleared off two shellings the extreme returnals from POSEN ALLEY on the left, later mad in Square H.31.a.53. The section is divided into 3 sub sections — No 6 Cameron Highlanders being on the left, No 8 Seaforth Highlanders on the right — into 3° manhaus given at intervals. The left of the firing line was held by "K" Coy, the centre by 1 platoon of "N" Coy, the right by 1st Coy. 3 platoons "M" Coy in support "L" Coy in Reserve. Battalion Headquarters and Headquarters Coy. in LOOS at front G.36.a central. Bn. H.Q. in a big cellar quite heated from no stove, very comfortable. Rations come up in the transport to chemin CRUCIFIX CORNER in LOOS from G.29.d.62 a distance of 1500 yards in a straight line to the firing line. It takes if a whole company to carry rations from the Battalion, sometimes they have to make 2 journeys — luckily there is water in LOOS which decreases the work. The line held by the Battalion is 1500 yards long & the Bn. strength 400 rifles — they have to be present in the front line — much too long & extended.	Trench map 36.c N.W.3. Edition 6

Army Form C. 2118.

WAR DIARY
or
INTELLIGENCE SUMMARY.
(Erase heading not required.)

Instructions regarding War Diaries and Intelligence Summaries are contained in F. S. Regs., Part II. and the Staff Manual respectively. Title pages will be prepared in manuscript.

Place	Date	Hour	Summary of Events and Information	Remarks and references to Appendices
	1916			
TRENCHES	22 Feb		The LOOS appendices has it own garrison of 450 rifles Steward and 12 machine guns, found by the 1st Division. Those defences consist of 5 defended localities each capable of all round defence.	
			An officers patrol from "A" Coy was out to reconnoitre old trench at A.25 d 49. I heard an enemy listening post.	
			All night rifle machine gun fire was opened on enemy working parties. Snow continued to fall. I there was no thaw. Wind NE to E. Enemy very quiet.	
- do -	23 Feb		During day fire opened on many German working parties, which were dispersed. At 7.15 a.m. 6 Germans shot – they were working on their parapet about 50 yards E. of LENS – LA BASSEE road I received absolutely indifferent to our fire. being seen working all night in their front trench.	
			An officers patrol went out at night & reconnoitred the barricade on the LENS road & found it composed of French wire & heavaux de frise I many easily removable, though the rest of the wire is very strong. Snow thaw in - moonlight made patrolling difficult.	

T.1134. Wt. W708-776. 500000. 4/15. Sir J. C. & 8.

Army Form C. 2118.

WAR DIARY
or
INTELLIGENCE SUMMARY.
(Erase heading not required.)

Instructions regarding War Diaries and Intelligence Summaries are contained in F. S. Regs., Part II. and the Staff Manual respectively. Title pages will be prepared in manuscript.

Place	Date 1916	Hour	Summary of Events and Information	Remarks and references to Appendices
TRENCHES	24 Feb.		Snow still on ground. No signs of thaw. Working parties of enemy on LENS Road again dispersed by rifle & machine gun fire. Our parapet was traversed by machine gun fire at night.	
		7.15am	Several Germans again working on top of their parapet near LENS Road – they were more cautious than yesterday, only one was killed.	
		7.0pm	An officer's patrol was out at night & found that during the last month the Battalion was in this part of the line a great deal of work has been done by the enemy – new trenches – reconnoitring was difficult owing to the crisp snow.	
do —	25 Feb.		Snow still on the ground. No signs of thaw. 1st — having been reorganised that the Brigade had to march line to held to 14 his SECTOR has started by the left ensuring on POSEN ALLEY its right on LOOS - ST LAURENT Road. The front allotted to the Battalion was about 800 yards. CHALK PIT ALLEY on left to the portion of the Coy. remained the same as far as the firing line. Supports & reserves were concerned, they simply moved down to them anyhow.	
			SCOTS ALLEY on right.	

WAR DIARY or INTELLIGENCE SUMMARY

Army Form C. 2118.

Place	Date	Hour	Summary of Events and Information	Remarks and references to Appendices
TRENCHES	25 Feb 1916		The 9th Black Watch came in on our left relieving the 7th Cameron Highlanders. The 8th Seaforth Highlanders were still on our right, but with a smaller front.	
		4 pm	Before the relief the enemy bombarded our line for about 100 yards E. of LENS square H 25 b with rifle grenades & trench mortars. Considerable damage was done to the trench of a 9th Black Watch working gun was unmarked. 1 man killed & several did both 9th R.W. — our casualties 3 Stretcher bearers rather shaken 4 of our men were sitting in a shelter, which was destroyed by a rifle grenade, but the reportedthatvery they weren't hurt. Have enemy working parties heard at night — no patrolling done. Thaw started in the late morning, but was not very rapid.	
— do —	26 Feb		Ground very much frightfully difficult — but although cold it is better than it will be when ground gets really slippy. Wind E to SE so gas about still continues, however more sentries & gas many shells fall into LOOS, but they do no harm to anyone set an only knock down houses. Sir Kipps the shells away from the trenches	

WAR DIARY
or
INTELLIGENCE SUMMARY.

(Erase heading not required.)

Army Form C. 2118.

Instructions regarding War Diaries and Intelligence Summaries are contained in F. S. Regs., Part II. and the Staff Manual respectively. Title pages will be prepared in manuscript.

Place	Date	Hour	Summary of Events and Information	Remarks and references to Appendices
TRENCHES	26.2d 1916		The usual clearing up went on in the afternoon. Patrols from "K" Coy. were out at 9.15pm to 2pm. At night a great deal of enemy working was heard & working parties were fired on by our artillery & also by machine guns.	
		10.15am	Our front support trench was shelled but very little damage done.	
		4.0pm	The shelling was probably caused by the RE carrying parties along the trench & leaving planks stack lying about. The RE are making a machine gun emplacement, which has already been spotted & shelled.	
do	27.2d		A German was shot at & seen to start to this morning. A good many heavy shells again fell at LOOS about 5 & 6 am. The shelling was kept up continuously all day. Enemy artillery on the whole more active, and to front support & reserve line. RAILWAY ALLEY were shelled with "whizz bangs" & rolly beans. Lieutenant J. Irvine was trampled — through in our line, an officer was wounded, Sergeant killed, 7 to 7 Cameron Highlanders machine gun. The front & rear trenches. The wind changed to S. Gas alert cancelled.	

Army Form C. 2118.

WAR DIARY
or
INTELLIGENCE SUMMARY.
(Erase heading not required.)

Instructions regarding War Diaries and Intelligence Summaries are contained in F. S. Regs., Part II. and the Staff Manual respectively. Title pages will be prepared in manuscript.

Place	Date	Hour	Summary of Events and Information	Remarks and references to Appendices
Tracing from Trench Map - Sheet 36c N.W.3 Ed.b $\frac{1}{10000}$				
LINE HELD BY BATTALION				
	21/2/16 - 25/2/16	Ⓐ to Ⓑ	1500 yards	
		Ⓒ to Ⓐ	800 "	
	26/2/16 - 2/3/16			
CENTRE SUB SECTION				
PUITS 14 BIS SECTION				

Army Form C. 2118.

WAR DIARY
or
INTELLIGENCE SUMMARY.
(Erase heading not required.)

Instructions regarding War Diaries and Intelligence Summaries are contained in F. S. Regs., Part II. and the Staff Manual respectively. Title pages will be prepared in manuscript.

Place	Date 1916	Hour	Summary of Events and Information	Remarks and references to Appendices
TRENCHES	27 Feb.		Work in trenches increased 100 per cent. as the frost binds the earth & the thaw loosens it, so that the sides of the trenches are always slipping in. Patrols at night report seeing much German working in his front trench. A listening patrol & 3 reconnoitring patrols were out at 7.30 – 8.30 p.m. 2/Lt. Munro Warren. 2/Lt. S. "M" Coy. patrol 2/Lt. Copeland + Pte Heggerty.	
— to —	28 Feb.		Gas alert cancelled in forenoon, but was to be put on later as wind changed to S.E. No effort of the snow & frost followed by the sudden thaw was beginning to be felt on the trenches, the sides of which fell in continuously & make a mud fire to any depth at the bottom — traverses & parapets too are shaky also fall in — it means indebted work for all ranks. Our trenches were intermittently shelled but only material damage done, no man hit. The enemy's snipers changed place in the evening. "M" & "L" moving up into the firing line "K" moving back into Support "I" into reserve. Patrols were put out at night, but reported very little enemy work. Loos was shelled intermittently all day, but little damage done.	

WAR DIARY or INTELLIGENCE SUMMARY

Army Form C. 2118.

Place	Date	Hour	Summary of Events and Information	Remarks and references to Appendices
TRENCHES	29/11 1916		Trenches in a very bad state. A good deal of mud & dirt preventing much cleaning. The Support & Reserve trenches had fallen in in several places. A sniper's post was constructed at the "dumbell" H316/H317. An enemy observation balloon was seen to track away spare men lines. Intermittent shelling all day - night very quiet. Officers patrols were out at night - "L" Coy. Capt. F.J.C. MOFFAT & 2nd Lieut. McLEAN. "M" Coy. Lieut. L.G. ROBERTSON, Capt. J. TURNER, 1/Cpl. J. CALDER. The enemy were not doing much work, but were laying a trolley line occasionally. The enemy fired two rifles at about a yards distance from each other, directly into the air - this must be some sort of signal.	

Army Form C. 2118.

WAR DIARY
or
INTELLIGENCE SUMMARY.
(Erase heading not required.)

Instructions regarding War Diaries and Intelligence Summaries are contained in F. S. Regs., Part II. and the Staff Manual respectively. Title pages will be prepared in manuscript.

Place	Date	Hour	Summary of Events and Information	Remarks and references to Appendices
	1916			
February	29		During the month the following officers were struck off the strength being invalided to England	
			Lieut. E.W. HANCOCK 27.1.16	
			" G.C. HOLLAND 14.2.16	
			2 " C.V. ROBERTSON 17.2.16	
			" W. McINTYRE 16.2.16	
			Officer transferred to A/94 Trench Mortar Battery	
			2 Lieut. R.H. COOPER 7.2.16	
			The following officers were promoted, the Gazettes appearing in February -	
			Lieut. A.P. BETHELL to be Captain 5.11.15	
			" J.G. PATERSON — do — 23.11.15	
			2 " T.B.G. McKENZIE to be Lieutenant 21.9.15	
			" L.G. ROBERTSON " " 26.9.15	
			" A INGLIS " " 5.11.15	
			" J.B. WOOD " " 23.11.15	
			Officer on sick leave, still on strength -	
			Lieut. F.W. GORDON 2 Lieut. P.W. SCOTT	

T./134. Wt. W708—776. 500000. 4/15. Sr J. C. & S.

Army Form C. 2118.

WAR DIARY
or
INTELLIGENCE SUMMARY.
(Erase heading not required.)

Instructions regarding War Diaries and Intelligence Summaries are contained in F.S. Regs., Part II. and the Staff Manual respectively. Title pages will be prepared in manuscript.

Place	Date	Hour	Summary of Events and Information	Remarks and references to Appendices
January	1916 29		Strength of Battalion — 29 Officers 777 other ranks ——— 806 Some drafts to make up to strength are very badly needed. Of the Battalion strength shewn we are normally available for duties in the trench shewing where the men are. Taken from log returns on 27/2/1916. Actually in trenches with the Battalion 16 officers 430 other ranks.	
			Not with the Battalion <table><tr><td></td><td>Off</td><td>O.R.</td><td></td><td>Off</td><td>O.R.</td></tr><tr><td>Transport</td><td>1</td><td>55</td><td>On leave</td><td>4</td><td>34</td><td>Attd. Bde. & Div.</td></tr><tr><td>Machine Gun Section</td><td>2</td><td>57</td><td>Quartermaster Stores</td><td>1</td><td>8</td><td>Shown above</td></tr><tr><td>— do — Company</td><td></td><td>7</td><td>Bombing School</td><td></td><td>18</td><td>water duties</td></tr><tr><td>— do — Course</td><td>2</td><td>8</td><td>Attd. Salvage Coy.</td><td></td><td>6</td><td>D.R. Sgt. Armourer Sgt.</td></tr><tr><td>Trench mortar Batteries</td><td></td><td>15</td><td>Cooks</td><td></td><td>7</td><td>Miscellaneous</td></tr><tr><td>Attached 253rd Coy R.E.</td><td></td><td>13</td><td>C.Q.M.S. & Storemen</td><td></td><td>7</td><td></td></tr><tr><td>On Command</td><td>3</td><td>26</td><td>Sick</td><td></td><td>17</td><td></td></tr><tr><td>Hospital</td><td>2</td><td>44</td><td>Ration party</td><td></td><td>21</td><td></td></tr><tr><td></td><td></td><td></td><td></td><td>15</td><td>376</td><td></td></tr></table>	16 430 With Battalion 15 376 Not with Battalion 31 806

Army Form C. 2118.

WAR DIARY
or
INTELLIGENCE SUMMARY.
(Erase heading not required.)

Instructions regarding War Diaries and Intelligence Summaries are contained in F. S. Regs., Part II. and the Staff Manual respectively. Title pages will be prepared in manuscript.

Place	Date	Hour	Summary of Events and Information	Remarks and references to Appendices
	1916			
February	29		Casualties during month —	
			Killed in action 6	
			Wounded — " — 21	
			— " — (at duty) 3	
			Sent to hospital 85	
			Total 115	
			Wounded (at duty) 3	
			Returned wounded 6	
			" hospital 27	
			36	
			Total loss 79	

W. M. Cuthbert Lt-Colonel
Comdg. 10th Gordon Highlanders
29/2/1916

T2134. Wt. W708—776. 500000. 4/15. Sir J. C. & S.

PLAN OF FIRE TRENCH
HELD BY
10TH GORDON HIGHLANDERS

Scale 1 inch = 100 yds

From Diary 10th Gordons, Feb. 1916

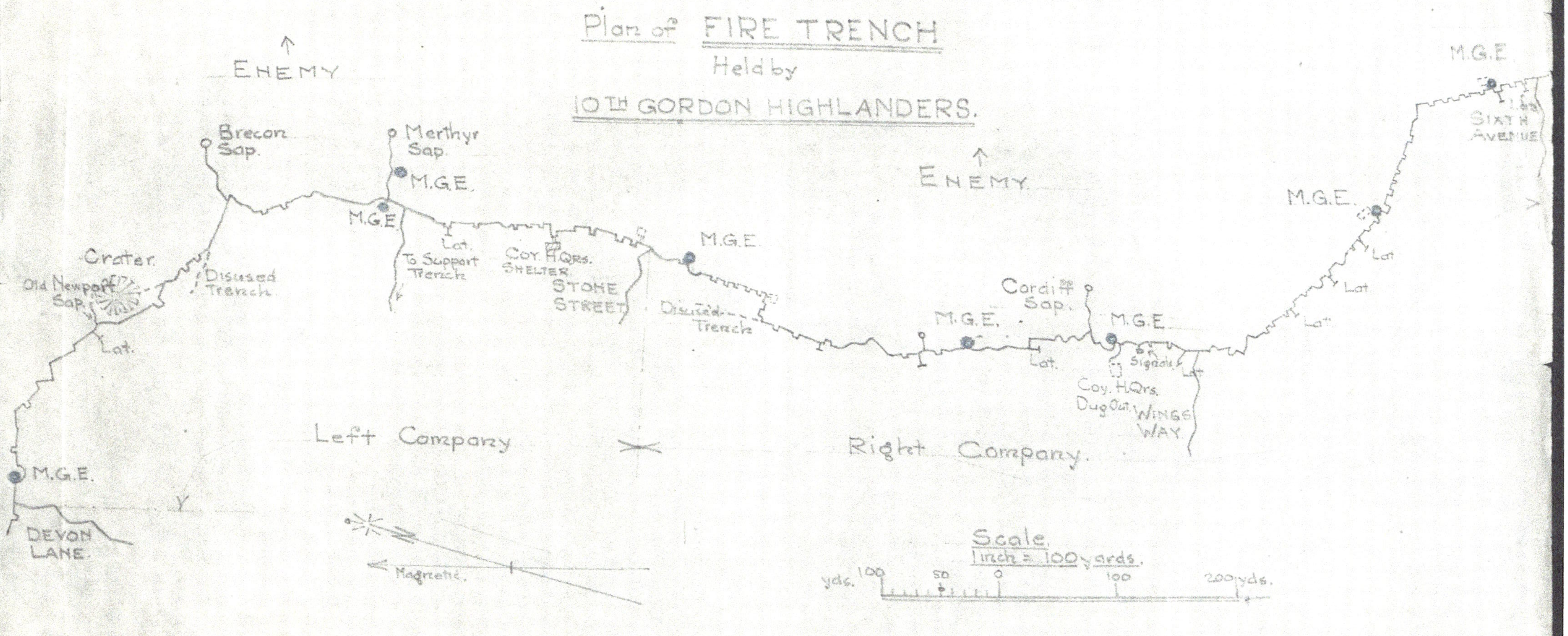
Plan of FIRE TRENCH
Held by
10TH GORDON HIGHLANDERS.
ENEMY
ENEMY
Brecon Sap.
Merthyr Sap.
M.G.E.
M.G.E.
Crater.
Old Newport Sap.
Disused Trench
Lat.
To Support Trench
Coy. H.Qrs. SHELTER
STONE STREET
M.G.E.
Disused Trench
M.G.E.
Cordiff Sap.
M.G.E.
Lat.
Signals
Coy. H.Qrs. Dug Out.
WINGS WAY
Lat
Lat
Lat
M.G.E.
M.G.E.
SIXTH AVENUE
Left Company
Right Company.
M.G.E.
DEVON LANE.
Magnetic.
Scale.
1 inch = 100 yards.
yds. 100
50
0
100
200 yds.
RF

Army Form C. 2118.

From Diary 10th Gordons Feb. 1916

WAR DIARY
or
INTELLIGENCE SUMMARY.
(Erase heading not required.)

Instructions regarding War Diaries and Intelligence Summaries are contained in F. S. Regs., Part II. and the Staff Manual respectively. Title pages will be prepared in manuscript.

Place	Date	Hour	Summary of Events and Information	Remarks and references to Appendices

LEFT SUB SECTION HULLUCH SECTION

Tracing from Trench Map 36c N.W.3 Edition 6 Scale 1/10000

HULLUCH ROAD — Bn. H.Q. — 10ᵗʰ AVENUE — RESERVE TRENCH — DEVON LANE — LE RUTOIRE ALLEY — HAY ALLEY — STONE ST. — Gd. 18 NEWPORT SAP — BEACON SAP — MERTHYR SAP — CARDIFF SAP — H.13a.11 — SUPPORT TRENCH — 6ᵗʰ AVENUE — FIRE TRENCH — GERMAN LINES — ST. ELIE — HULLUCH

T.2134. Wt. W708—776. 500000. 4/15. Sir J. C. & S.

Army Form C. 2118.

WAR DIARY
or
INTELLIGENCE SUMMARY.
(Erase heading not required.)

Instructions regarding War Diaries and Intelligence Summaries are contained in F. S. Regs., Part II. and the Staff Manual respectively. Title pages will be prepared in manuscript.

Place	Date	Hour	Summary of Events and Information	Remarks and references to Appendices

T/134. Wt. W708—776. 500000. 4/15. Sir J. C. & S.

WAR DIARY
or
INTELLIGENCE SUMMARY

Army Form C. 2118.

Place	Date	Hour	Summary of Events and Information	Remarks and references to Appendices
	1916			
	1 Feb.		Officers who have served with the 10th Gordon Highlanders since its arrival in France.	
			Lieut. Colonel STEWART MACDOUGALL — Killed 21.7.15.	
			" H.R. WALLACE — Sick leave 6.12.15	
			" W.W. MACGREGOR — Joined 28.1.16	
			Major A.H. FARQUHARSON — to 11th Batt. Gordon Hrs. 21.10.15	
			" C.J.M. CRICHTON — Killed 25.9.15	
			" H.K. LONGMAN — 2nd in command vice Major Farquharson attached 15th Divn. O.T.S. from 28.1.16.	
			Captain A.W. ANGUS —	
			" N.G. PEARSON — Wounded 3.12.15. To England.	
			" J.G. THOM —	
			" G.W.G. SUTHERLAND — Permanent Commission 1st Gordon Highrs. as 2nd Lieut. 24/11/15. (still with 10th Batt.)	
			" R.G. LONGMAN — To England.	
			" F.J.C. MOFFAT — Wounded 28.8.15. To England.	

Army Form C. 2118.

WAR DIARY
or
INTELLIGENCE SUMMARY.
(Erase heading not required.)

Instructions regarding War Diaries and Intelligence Summaries are contained in F. S. Regs., Part II. and the Staff Manual respectively. Title pages will be prepared in manuscript.

Place	Date	Hour	Summary of Events and Information	Remarks and references to Appendices
			Lieutenant T.H.B. VADE WALPOLE — Killed 20.9.15	
			" R.L. WATSON — Wounded 25.9.15 To England.	
			Captain A.B. BETHELL — Attached 15th Divn. b.T.S.	
			Lieutenant J.D. LAMMIE — Sick leave from 12.8.15	
			" R.C. CHRISTISON — Wounded & missing 25.9.15	
			" E.W. HANCOCK — Sick leave from 27.1.16	
			Captain C.G. HARPER —	
			Lieutenant J.G. PATERSON — Joined 30.8.15, sick leave from 9.2.16	
			" G.C. HOLLAND — appointed Adjutant 2.11.15 sick leave from	
			" F.W. GORDON — Wounded 25.9.15 To England	
			2nd " G.W. SYME — Transport Officer.	
			" T.B.G. McKENZIE — Wounded 25.9.15 To England.	
			Lieutenant G.J.S. LUMSDEN —	
			2nd " L.C. ROBERTSON — Signalling officer	
			" P.B. BOYD —	
			Lieutenant J.B. WOOD —	

WAR DIARY
or
INTELLIGENCE SUMMARY.
(Erase heading not required.)

Army Form C. 2118.

Place	Date	Hour	Summary of Events and Information	Remarks and references to Appendices
			Lieutenant A. INGLIS — Brigade Bombing Officer	
			2" J.S. HUSBAND — Machine Gun Officer	
			" G.S. MILNE — Joined 5.10.15	
			" A.F. SPROTT — " 7.10.15 wounded 29.11.15 rejoined 15.2.16	
			" G.R.W. STEWART — " 7.10.15 To A44 Light Trentin Batty. 30.11.15	
			" W.L. McLEAN — " 10.10.15 Reserve M.G. Officer	
			" G. ROBERTSON — " 10.10.15 killed 17.11.15	
			" J.E. LAW — " 13.10.15	
			" A.N. BAIN — " 13.10.15	
			" P.W. SCOTT — " 5.11.15 Sick leave from 10.2.16	
			" W. McINTYRE — " 12.12.15 — do. — 10.2.16	
			" R.A.M. BLACK — " 17.12.15	
			" R.M. RIDDEL — " 18.12.15	
			" R.A. COOPER — " 13.12.15 To B 44 Light Trentin Batty 14.1.16	
			" J.S. SEMPLE — " 23.12.15	
			" C.V. ROBERTSON — " 30.12.15 Sick leave from 22.1.16	
			" H.R. KNOWLES — " 2.1.16	

44

10^t Jackey
V6T9

Army Form C. 2118.

WAR DIARY
or
INTELLIGENCE SUMMARY.
(Erase heading not required.)

Instructions regarding War Diaries and Intelligence Summaries are contained in F. S. Regs., Part II. and the Staff Manual respectively. Title pages will be prepared in manuscript.

Place	Date	Hour	Summary of Events and Information	Remarks and references to Appendices
TRENCHES	1916 March 1		The enemy made our new front trench stand-until renewed shelling - a few more casualties - but considering the numbers of shells fired - even the number of men hit is very small. The trenches took a great deal of work clearing up after the thaw. In the late afternoon & early evening & at 9.30 a.m. our trenches were shelled by field guns - heavy and very searching - parties were sent-at-night-they were dispersed by rifle & machine gun & unwilling fire but-needs many flare-lights - it seems as if PUITS 14 BIS was being made into a strong point. 31 boxes of ammunition were brought-to CRUCIFIX CORNER at-night & carried up to the firing line - this in addition to the rations meant that the whole companies were employed in carrying. The Battalion has used about 2000 sandbags in the last 24 hours revetting & refacing damage caused by the snow & frost & thaw. Pte F.W. GORDON was struck off the strength for a machine gun hand. F.W. Scott found "unfit-to return" by a medical board, struck off strength 2/3/16.	
" "	2 March		2nd Lieut. F.W. Scott found "unfit-to return" by a medical board, struck off strength 2/3/16.	

Army Form C. 2118.

WAR DIARY
or
INTELLIGENCE SUMMARY.
(*Erase heading not required.*)

Instructions regarding War Diaries and Intelligence Summaries are contained in F. S. Regs., Part II. and the Staff Manual respectively. Title pages will be prepared in manuscript.

Place	Date	Hour	Summary of Events and Information	Remarks and references to Appendices
	1916			
TRENCHES	2 Mar.		During the evening of 1st - 2nd "K" Companies RAILWAY ALLEY was quite clean in the morning, but bath has not been turn between of CHALK PIT ALLEY. Nothing of much importance to record - a glorious sunny spring morning. Enemy started shelling LOOS about 5 a.m. but seem to have ceased his idea fly. In the morning the 46th Infantry Brigade relieved the 44th Infantry Brigade. Battalion was relieved by the 10th Scottish Rifles. The guides met the incoming Battalion at PHILOSOPHE cross roads at 6.0 p.m. & brought them via LOOS & man lead to RAILWAY ALLEY. The relief worked very smoothly & was completed by 8.40 p.m. The Battalion moved out via CHALK PIT ALLEY to 10th AVENUE & thence	
NOEUX LES MINES	3rd Mar.	2.0 a.m.	across country to Lillers in NOEUX - LES - MINES. A long way in "1" Coy. arrived about 2.0 a.m. the others about 3.0 a.m. The arrival was even quieter than any earlier - but it was ready for steam from vans of dram & bread were brought out by the Canteen fund. A day of rest - About 2 p.m. gas alert - heavy rain in evening.	

WAR DIARY
or
INTELLIGENCE SUMMARY.

Army Form C. 2118.

Place	Date	Hour	Summary of Events and Information	Remarks and references to Appendices
	1916			
			Casualties during time 19th Feb. to 2nd March —	
			Killed in action 2	
			Wounded " " — 7	The outstanding feature of the time was 12 Coys lives deep in the trenches — 3 in support, 9 in the firing line.
			" at duty 4	
			Sent to Hospital 33	
			Total 46	
			Wounded at duty 4	
			Retd. from Hosp. 3 7	
			Total done 39	
NOEUX LES MINES	4 Mar		Heavy snow in morning — hard freezing, 30 recruits in a filthy state. Most of the blankets of the Battalion were fumigated. The usual inspecting parties to be found daily from washer the Town Major for clearing the streets: 1 N.C.O. + 12 men at 8.30 am + 2.0 pm. 42 mouth organs were issued to Battalion: each one was plainly marked "MADE IN GERMANY" !!! but they are fine instruments "The Cornet-à-band" or "Noah's Ark".	

Army Form C. 2118.

WAR DIARY
or
INTELLIGENCE SUMMARY.
(Erase heading not required.)

Instructions regarding War Diaries and Intelligence Summaries are contained in F. S. Regs., Part II. and the Staff Manual respectively. Title pages will be prepared in manuscript.

Place	Date 1916	Hour	Summary of Events and Information	Remarks and references to Appendices
NOEUX LES MINES	4 Mar		Extract from London Gazette dated 3rd March 1916 — GORD. HIGHRS. — Temp. Lt. Col. H.R. WALLACE (Hon. Maj. late (S.R.) Arg. and Suth'd Highldrs.) relinquishes temp. commn. on ceasing to command a Bn. (March 4)	
—do—	5 Mar		The Divisional Baths were at the disposal of the Battalion.	
	Sunday		Church Parades. Presbyterians 10 a.m. in Cinema shed (The patrons standing just outside a hazing ring that has been used the night before). Church of England Holy Commn 9 am. service 11 am. Divisional Recreation Room. Roman Catholic — parish church 12 noon. A gas demonstration was held at —12.15 p.m. for the Battalion — Whistles were put on men rattles through the gas.	
			Capt. THOM next to a machine gun course.	
—do—	6 Mar		Working parties were found as under —	
		8.30 am	2 officers + 100 men under 216th A.T. Coy R.E. at MAZINGARBE.	
		8.0 am	1 " 75 " — do —	
		6 pm	2 " 100 " 73rd Co. R.E.	
			2 " 100 " 91st Co. R.E.	
			2 " 100 " 74th Co R.E.	

Army Form C. 2118.

WAR DIARY
or
INTELLIGENCE SUMMARY.
(Erase heading not required.)

Instructions regarding War Diaries and Intelligence
Summaries are contained in F. S. Regs., Part II.
and the Staff Manual respectively. Title pages
will be prepared in manuscript.

Place	Date	Hour	Summary of Events and Information	Remarks and references to Appendices
	1916			
NOEUX LES MINES	6 Jun		heavy snow shower in morning, followed by snow — A return sent to the Brigade showed the numbers who had not been on leave as —	
			Over 6 months in the country 188	
			Between 5 & 6 months —do— 80	
			„ 4 & 5 „ —do— 44	
			„ 3 & 4 „ —do— 27	

T.J.134. Wt. W708—776. 500000. 4/15. Sir J. C. & S.

WAR DIARY or INTELLIGENCE SUMMARY

Army Form C. 2118.

Place	Date 1916	Hour	Summary of Events and Information	Remarks and references to Appendices
NOEUX LES MINES	7 Mar		Wet & raining all day. Working parties & officers two O.R. under R.E. in Pioneers as usual; but there has been middle strong rain; never got to the right places.	
to			Rain changed into snow & we made to fine country quite white.	
TRENCHES	8 Mar		4th Brigade relieved 45th Brigade in the HULLUCH SECTOR Trenches. The Battalion relieved the 6th Cameron Highlanders in the entire sub section HULLUCH Sector — from LE AVENUE having NOEUX LES MINES at 8.30 am traversing via MAZINGARBE PHILOSOPHE & VERMELLES on left & VENDIN ALLEY to right. The relief was reported complete at 1.40 pm.	LE AVENUE on left to VENDIN ALLEY on right.
			The day fine — but the trenches very muddy from melting snow. On our right the 8th Seaforth Highlanders, on our left the 7th Cameron Highlanders. The relief worked smoothly & peacefully.	
— do —	9 Mar		Bright last night, chiefly clearing out trenches & a certain amount of wiring done in our right.	
			It has been decided that owing to the bad weather men were not to be in the trenches more than 9 days out of the 12 — to put this into effect — 1 Coy "I" to 9th Black Watch (Battalion in Brigade Support) relieves "K" Coy, the latter	

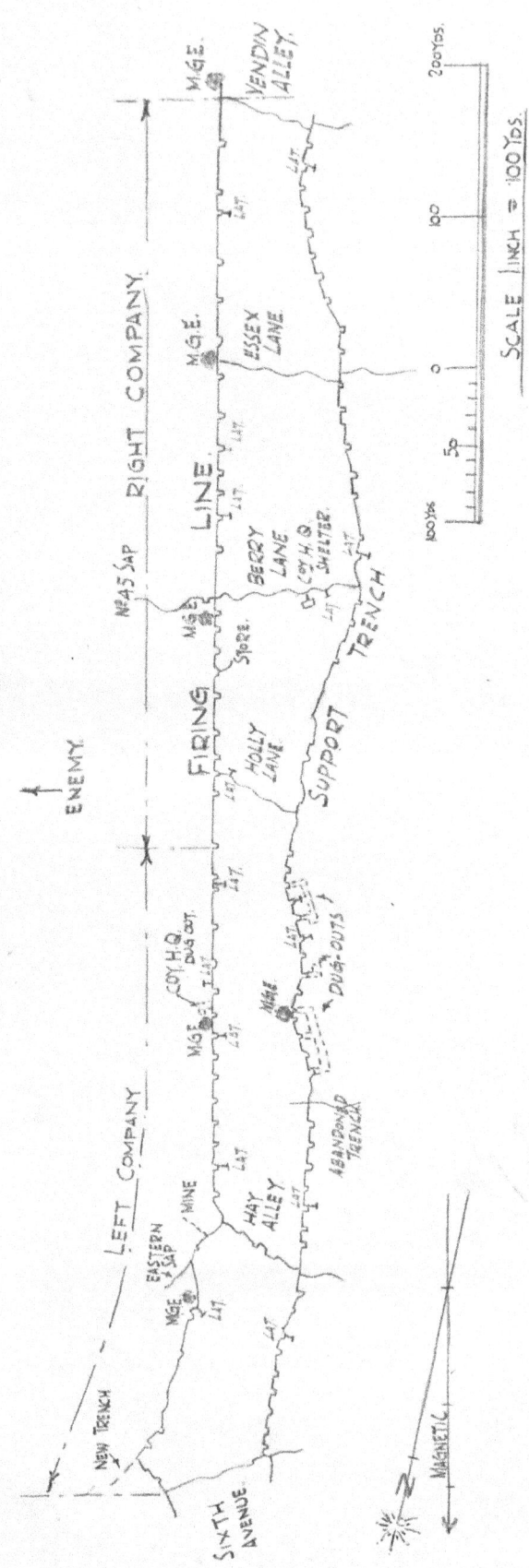

WAR DIARY or INTELLIGENCE SUMMARY.

Army Form C. 2118.

Place	Date	Hour	Summary of Events and Information	Remarks and references to Appendices
TRENCHES	1916 9th Mar.		Moving back into billets at PHILOSOPHE.	
			Captain C.N. COAD R.A.M.C. was sent on duty to be have absorbed new medical charge of the Battalion to Captain E.A. LUMLEY R.A.M.C. & this was confirmed as permanent on 16/3/16	
			The strength of the Battalion — numbers in trenches	
			H.Qrs Coy 2 Officers 56 men	
			"I" 2 " 105 "	
			"K" 2 " 103 "	
			"L" 3 " 89 "	
			"M" 2 " 110 "	
			Total 11 463	
			A great deal of work to be done clearing up trenches — snow upon straight trenches falling continually.	
			NORTHERN, SOUTHERN & NEW SAPS were deepened & cleared up.	
			"L" Coy did some wiring	
			Sniper located in tree opposite VENDIN ALLEY & made to descend at the double.	

Place	Date	Hour	Summary of Events and Information	Remarks and references to Appendices
TRENCHES	1916 9 Nov.		2nd Lt. BAIN M/G. THOMSON went out on patrol up Sap 45 - but enemy very careful - no tracks in front line to watch, brought enemy bag a front of 2 men on his lip. 2nd Lt. SEMPLE & Cpl. TURNER successfully FUSILIER CRATER opened no trace of a sap from enemy line heavily bombarded with rifle grenades in afternoon, but retaliation by our Artillery completed silenced enemy activity. No more grenades came over. Sounds of mining heard in deep dug out. 100 x S of HAY ALLEY.	
do	10		A draft of 82 other ranks arrived. 2Lt. P. BOYD went to the Army Signal School for a fortnight's course. In seven trot-full men rifle mallets & filled in trenches with water- the morning twelve rounds T.B.morning - but the snow melted it more. An unenjoyable quiet day - a mine blown up at 10 p.m. at night caused some activity, but it soon quieted down. 2nd Lt. LELAW went to hospital with appendicitis. 2nd Lt. C. HOGGE reported for duty with the Battalion on 9/2/16.	

Army Form C. 2118.

WAR DIARY
or
INTELLIGENCE SUMMARY.
(Erase heading not required.)

Instructions regarding War Diaries and Intelligence Summaries are contained in F. S. Regs., Part II. and the Staff Manual respectively. Title pages will be prepared in manuscript.

Place	Date 1916	Hour	Summary of Events and Information	Remarks and references to Appendices
TRENCHES	14 Mar.		A quiet night. A great deal of cleaning up of trenches to be done. Mining parties were out from "L" Coy. & wire in main family road between VENDIN ALLEY & SAP 45 — NORTHERN & SOUTHERN SAPS were also deepened & cleared. 2 Germans were shot at 7 am looking men moved out of craters into own trench.	
		1.30 pm	Enemy started bombarding our front line with 5.9" HE shells + heard on from an hour. The fire was concentrated on SOUTHERN SAP & firing line just at NE end of HAY ALLEY. SOUTHERN SAP was levelled & the firing line completely blocked. The enemy played in probably to destroy some mine shafts that were being made. The shelling stopped about 2.30 pm when the shelling started again. there were no casualties & only material damage done — Mr. SEMPLE, when the shelling started again the men out of the sap & away from the front of the line being shelled. In the afternoon about 4 pm "L" & "M" Coys. in the firing line were relieved by "A", "B" Coys. 8th Innistkilling Fusiliers & "L" & "M" Coys. moved down into billets at PHILOSOPHE. The Battalion in the centre sub section now consisted of 2 Coys. of 2nd Capt. K. Garden Highlanders — one in support, one in reserve. 2 Coys. 8th Innistkilling Fusiliers in the firing line.	

WAR DIARY or INTELLIGENCE SUMMARY

Army Form C. 2118.

Place	Date	Hour	Summary of Events and Information	Remarks and references to Appendices
TRENCHES	1915 11 Nov		The 8th Inniskilling Fusiliers belonged to the 16th Division & were sent into the trenches for training & instruction - this was their first night in the trenches as a Company. There was a great deal of noise before them in pulling up the firing line & clearing up SOUTHERN SAP - however they got on pretty well with it. & got the firing line through before daylight. It is thought that the Germans have rifles fixed on certain points at night, that a man spen round & fires them one after another. The Germans were slept early by the 8 Inniskillings.	
do	12 Nov		Then worked in clearing up & much improves the situation. There was an eventful day with a certain amount of machine gun fire into our lines. At night attempts to dig out SOUTHERN SAP were completely stopped by machine & rifle grenade fire. The men was also very bright, which made matters more uninteresting for us. Captain R.C. LONGMAN reported for duty with the Battalion. He had been wounded on 28/8/15. 2nd Lieut. D.C.F. ELLIOTT — do —	

Army Form C. 2118.

WAR DIARY
or
INTELLIGENCE SUMMARY.
(Erase heading not required.)

Instructions regarding War Diaries and Intelligence Summaries are contained in F. S. Regs., Part II. and the Staff Manual respectively. Title pages will be prepared in manuscript.

Place	Date	Hour	Summary of Events and Information	Remarks and references to Appendices
TRENCHES	13 June 1916		Nothing special to record. The troops (8th Inniskilling Fusiliers) seem alright, but result does not promise to Northern & Southern Saps show no signs of improvement.	
-do-	14 June		10th Gordon Highlanders took over left sub section HULLUCH SECTOR - their sub section now extends from STONE STREET to HAY ALLEY (incl. the 8th Seaforth Highlanders are to take over SOUTHERN SAP) In the firing line "L" Coy. on right "M" Coy. on left: "K" Coy. Support. "D" Coy. 8th Inniskilling Fusiliers in Reserve. The line has now been shortened & little attn 9th Batt. Royal Fusiliers 35th Brigade. 10th Division are now on our left; the divisions line being the HULLUCH ROAD. The centre sub section was taken over by the 8th Seaforth Highlanders who relieved "A" & "B" Coys 8th Inniskilling Fusiliers in the firing line who (these 2 Coys. moved into Reserve). "I" Coy. in Support (two Coys moved into do -- into 10th Avenue).	

Army Form C. 2118.

WAR DIARY
or
INTELLIGENCE SUMMARY.
(Erase heading not required.)

Instructions regarding War Diaries and Intelligence Summaries are contained in F. S. Regs., Part II. and the Staff Manual respectively. Title pages will be prepared in manuscript.

Place	Date	Hour	Summary of Events and Information	Remarks and references to Appendices
TRENCHES	1916 14 Mar		Lillers al- PHILOSOPHE:) "K" in Reserve (tin hay. moved into Support in left sub-section). An intense mine but everything worked well, & everyone soon settled down in their new places.	

Army Form C. 2118.

WAR DIARY
or
INTELLIGENCE SUMMARY.
(Erase heading not required.)

Place	Date	Hour	Summary of Events and Information	Remarks and references to Appendices
TRENCHES	1916 15th		Very great improvement in weather. Enemy pressure & trenches showing up nicely. In this section enemy very active with rifle grenades, there we fired men in relieves of 3 on 1 at a time, 2 are very annoying — 1 man killed & 2 wounded when our trenches were bombarded between 7 am & 8. to our own Support line; where unoccupied, was shelled by heavy shells between 12 noon & 1 pm.	
		9.0 pm	A small mine (100 lbs. gun cotton) was exploded by us., chiefly to withdraw enemy ranging. heavy arrangement was made & sentry the crater & holding parties of "L" Company detailed out. Immediately the explosion took place, but there was no cover and crater to be seen. Our stay here was not until a very heavy fire of rifle, rifle grenades & machine guns . they retired without casualties. the charge has not been big enough to make a big crater as the crown was very much broken up. it was found that the present safe were adequate; these were improved.	
			The Germans seemed to react - to explosion as directly it went off - a very heavy fire, rifles, rifle grenades, machine guns, & trench mortars was opened on	

Army Form C. 2118.

WAR DIARY
or
INTELLIGENCE SUMMARY.
(Erase heading not required.)

Instructions regarding War Diaries and Intelligence Summaries are contained in F. S. Regs., Part II. and the Staff Manual respectively. Title pages will be prepared in manuscript.

Place	Date	Hour	Summary of Events and Information	Remarks and references to Appendices
TRENCHES	1916 15 Thurs		our parapet — but no one was hit. Also only damage was to the arm by a rifle grenade, which did not explode; the arm is badly bruised. This is the 2nd case of the same kind that has happened in this Battalion. "L" Coy were to occupy the [manor] top of his crater, under command of Capt: MOFFAT. The rest of the night passed very quietly.	
— do —	16 Fri		Nothing very special happened. The day was fine. The Huns indulged in his usual pastime of sniping & rifle grenading our trenches. The new hostile grenade is really more an aerial dart — the body, like a rifle grenade, only much bigger, its fluid tail has three fins fixed on — it meant to find by a compressed air gun — luckily not many fall into our trench so do not do much harm. A regular bombardment with trench mortar darts took place between 12 midnight & 4 am. Our artillery were called in to help silence them, but were not successful	

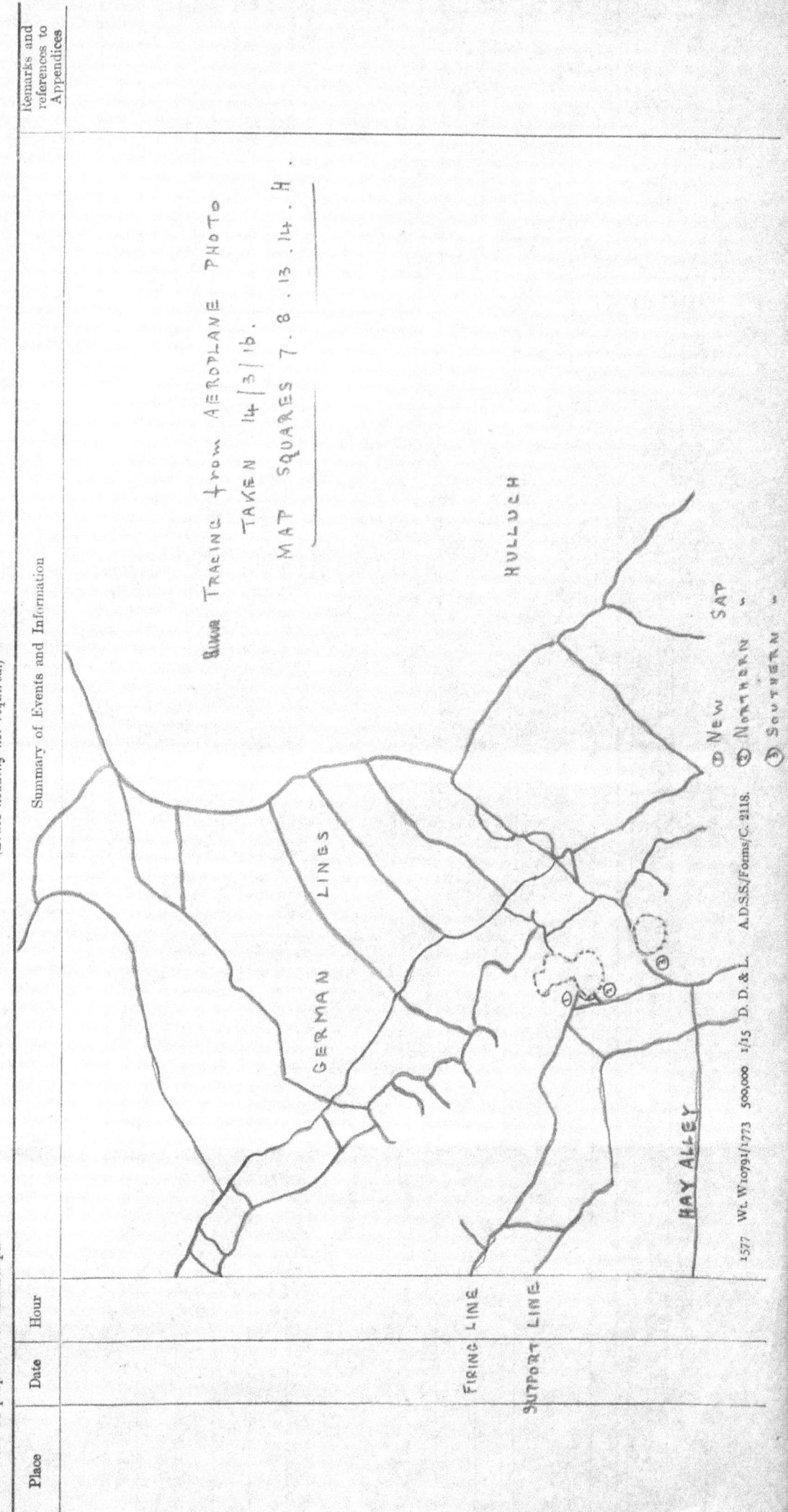

Instructions regarding War Diaries and Intelligence Summaries are contained in F. S. Regs., Part II. and the Staff Manual respectively. Title pages will be prepared in manuscript.

WAR DIARY
or
INTELLIGENCE SUMMARY.
(Erase heading not required.)

Army Form C. 2118.

Place	Date	Hour	Summary of Events and Information	Remarks and references to Appendices

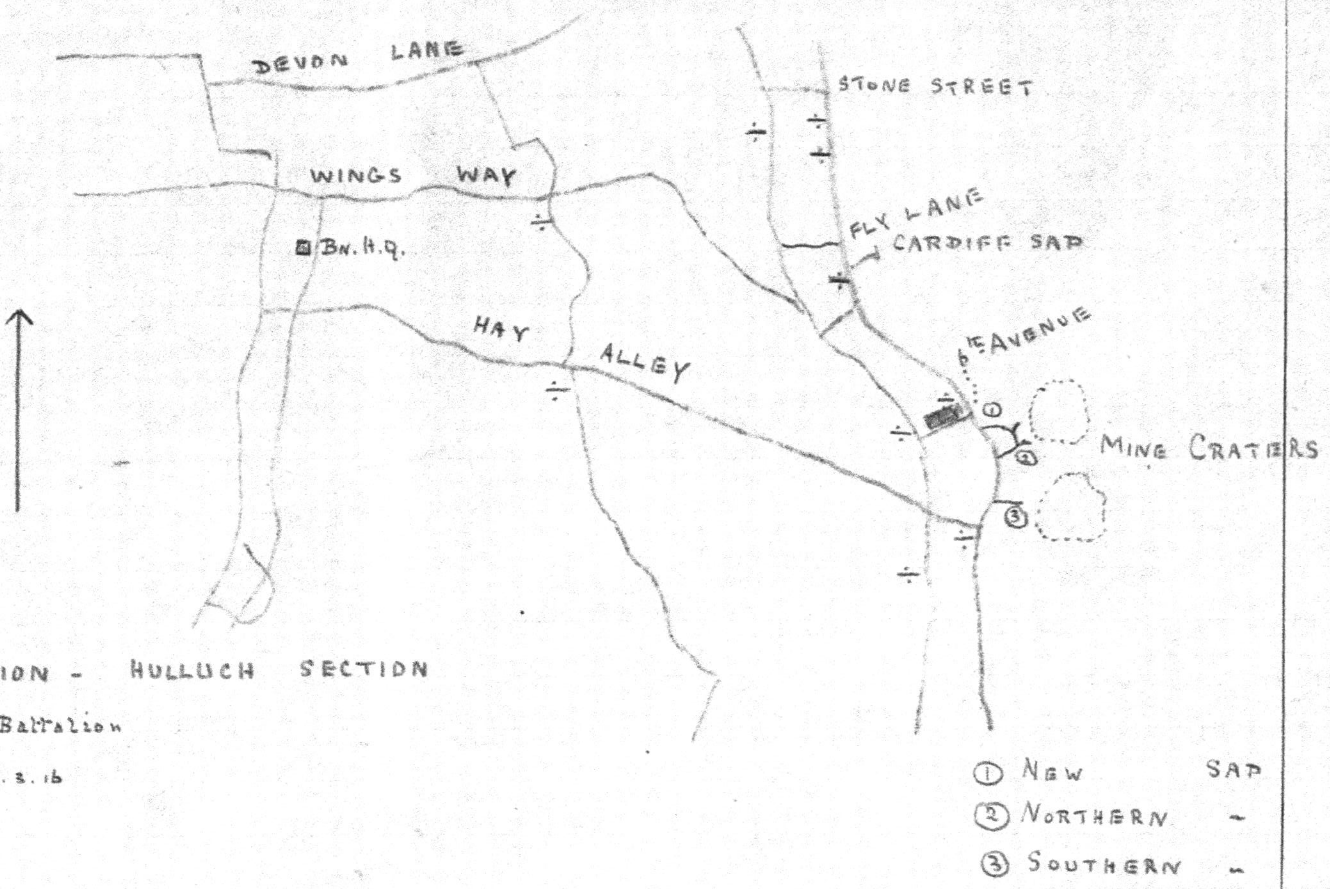

DEVON LANE
STONE STREET
WINGS WAY
BN. H.Q.
FLY LANE
CARDIFF SAP
HAY ALLEY
6th AVENUE
MINE CRATERS
① NEW SAP
② NORTHERN –
③ SOUTHERN –

LEFT SUB-SECTION – HULLUCH SECTION

occupied by the Battalion

14.3.16 – 20.3.16

1577 Wt. W10791/1773 500,000 1/15 D. D. & L. A.D.S.S./Forms/C. 2118.

WAR DIARY
or
INTELLIGENCE SUMMARY.

(Erase heading not required.)

Army Form C. 2118.

Place	Date	Hour	Summary of Events and Information	Remarks and references to Appendices
	1916			
	16 Mar.		Extract from the London Gazette dated 16.3.16 —	
			GORDON. H. — Temp. Lieut. Col. W.W. MACGREGOR. D.S.O. Royal H. 6th Lieut. Col. while commanding batt.	
			Jan. 28. Temp. Lieut. Col. W.W. MACGREGOR, D.S.O. temp. may to command batt., vice Temp.	
			Lieut. Col. H.R. WALLACE. March 4.	

Army Form C. 2118.

WAR DIARY
or
INTELLIGENCE SUMMARY.
(Erase heading not required.)

Place	Date	Hour	Summary of Events and Information	Remarks and references to Appendices
TRENCHES	1916 17 Mar		The chief feature of him time is the continual bombarding of our trenches by the arrival dents to supply of rifle grenades from us in very limited. The Germans is recent showers in dummy supplying himself with supper of destruction. The position of the Companies was changed today. The right of the firing line was taken over by "K" Coy. — "I" — (who took over Lillebis in PHILOSOPHE) — left — do — "M" Coy. went into support. "L" Coy. replaced "D" Coy. 8th Inniskilling Fusiliers in Reserve. The 8th Inniskilling Fusiliers was considered to the industrial stock over the right section of the HULLUCH Section, as a Battalion. At night "K" Coy. under Capt. THOM did most excellent work in joining up a new sap Northern Sap so made it more difficult for the enemy to envying the trench, which had been formed some time ago. 2nd Lieut. R.M. HOFFORD reported for duty with the Battalion.	

WAR DIARY
or
INTELLIGENCE SUMMARY.
(Erase heading not required.)

Army Form C. 2118.

Place	Date	Hour	Summary of Events and Information	Remarks and references to Appendices
TRENCHES	18 Mar. 1916		Intermittent rifle grenading all day. At 6 p.m. having exhausted our supply of rifle grenades & assisted by No 19 Trench Mortar Batty. & the R.F.A. a strafe was organised on the German line. Before our Trench Mortars were fired on, all of which burst short & several claimed 3 direct hits. Whatever the result was it seems to have upset the accuracy of the hostile rifle grenadiers whose accuracy has badly deteriorated. The R.F.A. could not help very much as an attack on the HOHENZOLLERN Redoubt division centres diverted their attention. The attack was on the line on our left held by the 12th Division; & although not much more than a mile away, the firing shells could be clearly seen absent on our front. If the line was properly quiet, except for our grenade strafe. Lieut. C.G. HARPER went to hospital sick.	

WAR DIARY or INTELLIGENCE SUMMARY.

(Erase heading not required.)

Army Form C. 2118.

Place	Date	Hour	Summary of Events and Information	Remarks and references to Appendices
	1916			
TRENCHES	19 Jan		A fine, moderate fine day. Between 5-6 pm he opened a rifle grenade strafe with very good effect. Every reply was futile; he was heard running about in trench refreshing ammunition as the our rifle grenades came over. At 10 pm a mine was exploded away on our left, but our front & the line was all peace.	
	20 Jan		The 44th Infantry Brigade units were relieved by the 46th Infantry Brigade in the HULLUCH SECTION. The Battalion was relieved by the 7th K.O.S.B. on temporary Guides over the incoming KOSB at 9.15 am — the Junction of Wives Way to AVIGNON the relief was complete about 11 am. The Battalion were rather slacked on its way out some shell came rather near but luckily no moves. It was a cloudy & a great fire wind relief. The Battalion moved into billets at NOEUX-LES-MINES, when they arrived	
NOEUX LES MINES			about 3 pm. Each Company being placed in by their own Subalterns & Officers. For 3 days "1" Coy had been on the left. "B" the line without a casualty, immediately the 7th K.O.S.B. took over they had no Officer & 2 men wounded by a rifle Grenade	

Army Form C. 2118.

WAR DIARY
or
INTELLIGENCE SUMMARY.
(*Erase heading not required.*)

Instructions regarding War Diaries and Intelligence Summaries are contained in F. S. Regs., Part II. and the Staff Manual respectively. Title pages will be prepared in manuscript.

Place	Date	Hour	Summary of Events and Information	Remarks and references to Appendices
March	1916 20		The chief features of the last term in the trenches were —	
			1. Enemy artillery with rifle grenades, which had to be met with like artillery.	
			2. The wind was in the E. nearly all the time, which meant continual gas alarms.	
			3. The thaw started in earnest & finished up in warm spring like sunny weather.	
			The casualties during the term 3rd to 20th March were —	
			O. O.R.	
			Killed in action 2	
			Wounded — — — 19	
			— (at duty) 0	
			Sent to Hospital 2 . 72	
			Total 93	
			Returned from Hospital 11	
			Total loss 2 . 82	
			N.B. 2 Killed & 6 wounded occurred with draft on 16th inst.	

Army Form C. 2118.

WAR DIARY
or
INTELLIGENCE SUMMARY.
(Erase heading not required.)

Instructions regarding War Diaries and Intelligence Summaries are contained in F. S. Regs., Part II. and the Staff Manual respectively. Title pages will be prepared in manuscript.

Place	Date	Hour	Summary of Events and Information	Remarks and references to Appendices
	1916			
NOEUX LES MINES	21 Mar		2nd Lt. J. MORRISON reported for duty with the Battalion. Major F. W. GORDON returned from sick leave, unexpectedly having been spared again after being cleared for nearly a recruit. Tuesday a draft of 11 N.C.O.s was arrived.	
— do —	22 Mar		The Platters were at the disposal of the Battalion for some part of the day. The blankets were disinfected at 10th	
— do —	23 Mar		The Battalion and Transport were inspected by the Commanding Officer & the men were very well turned out. A start was made in cleaning up the buttons, which is much added to the appearance generally. The Pipe Band in preparing & played 3 or 4 marches, up & down between itself. Extract from London gazette dated 10 March 1916 — "GORDON H. Temp Capt: A.W. ANGUS to be temp. maj. Nov. 5."	
— do —	24 Mar		A most astonishing change in the weather. One woke up to find the ground all white & snow still coming. The Brigade was to be inspected by the Army Commander etc. but the parade was cancelled.	

WAR DIARY or INTELLIGENCE SUMMARY

Place	Date	Hour	Summary of Events and Information	Remarks and references to Appendices
NOEUX LES MINES	25th Jan 1916		The Battalion paraded at 9.10 a.m. marched to the station entraining at 4 bore a being trained to LILLERS & from thence marching to billets at ALLOUAGNE.	
ALLOUAGNE			The 8th Seaforths & 7th Cameron Highlanders are also in billets at the same place. The Battalion were in the same billets as they were in at Xmas time. Captain DAWSON A.V.C. was attached to the Battalion for rations & forage for Headquarters.	
Sunday	26th		1st Corps Commander made customary attempt to inspect the Principals, but as it poured with rain the inspection was again postponed. Church Parades 11.20 a.m. Presbyterian. 11.15 a.m. Church of England. Certain statements were elicited for us 4 horses of the Battalion transport & section to Garden Highlanders, all statements not marked were furnished by Hounds.	
	27th		Platoon Training commenced. While the bombs were being inspected, a strike became loose & one bomb exploded, 3 men were slightly wounded.	

WAR DIARY
or
INTELLIGENCE SUMMARY.
(Erase heading not required.)

Army Form C. 2118.

Place	Date	Hour	Summary of Events and Information	Remarks and references to Appendices
ALLOUAGNE	1916 28 Mar		The 4th Punjabs marched into LILLERS & were inspected by General Sir Charles Monro Commanding First Army. The Punjabs looked very well on parade. The Army Commander made a speech, but the wind made it very difficult to hear. The Punjabs then marched home in pouring rain giving three cheers. Captain R.G. LONGMAN having resumed from a course at GOSNAY took over command of "M" Company. Captain J.G. PATERSON being transferred to "K" Coy. The ladies at AUCHEL have open to the Battalion today.	
"	29 Mar		A draft of 53 N.C.O's men arrived today. They were equipped complete in every way.	
"	30 "		Glorious sunny weather - platoon training carried on. The following classes were carried on:- 50 N.C.O's men in Lewis gun Wthin rectic team Signallers Snipers Musketry on 30 yards range. Assault Course	

Army Form C. 2118.

WAR DIARY
or
INTELLIGENCE SUMMARY.
(Erase heading not required.)

Place	Date	Hour	Summary of Events and Information	Remarks and references to Appendices
	1916			
	31 March		Strength of Battalion - 33 Officers / 844 Other Ranks / 877	
			Casualties during month	
			Killed 3	
			Wounded 23	
			" at duty 3	
			" accid 3 / 32	
			" natal 1 / 31	
			Sick to Hospital — Officers 2 / Other Ranks 5 / 116	
			Returned — 1 / 43 / 4 / 73	
			6 Officers joined on appointment	
			149 Other Ranks joined in drafts	
			Lt Col upson Lt Colonel to Gordon Highlanders	

WAR DIARY
INTELLIGENCE SUMMARY

Date April 1916

War Diary
of
1st/6th Bn Gordon Highlanders
From
1st to 30th April 1916.

Army Form C. 2118.

WAR DIARY
or
INTELLIGENCE SUMMARY.
(Erase heading not required.)

Instructions regarding War Diaries and Intelligence Summaries are contained in F. S. Regs., Part II. and the Staff Manual respectively. Title pages will be prepared in manuscript.

Place	Date 1916	Hour	Summary of Events and Information	Remarks and references to Appendices
ALLOUAGNE	1 April		Company Training starts today and was carried on until the G.O.C. went training programme & between & great stress was laid by him on the authorities on the value of ceremonial. Major-General (Temp.Lieut.General) C.T. McM. KAVANAGH C.V.O. C.B. D.S.O. assumed Command of the 1st Corps today.	
do	2. Sunday		8 Classes of 30 men per Coy commenced in writing were carried on under instruction from 9. Gordon Highlanders. Church parades Church of England 11.45 am. Presbyterian 10.45 am R.C. 11.45 in the Village Church.	
	3.		The Iron instruments (travis packs, as the men call them) were taken in today in baths at AUCHEL were allotted to the Battalion.	
	4.		A Company Football league was carried on & decided which was the best Company for the Inter Battalion leg competition.	
	5.		A Football match played against the 8th Seaforth Highlanders resulted in a win for 10th Gordon Highlanders winning by 2 goals to nil.	

Army Form C. 2118

WAR DIARY
or
INTELLIGENCE SUMMARY

(Erase heading not required.)

Instructions regarding War Diaries and Intelligence Summaries are contained in F. S. Regs., Part II. and the Staff Manual respectively. Title Pages will be prepared in manuscript.

Place	Date 1916	Hour	Summary of Events and Information	Remarks and references to Appendices
ALLOUAGNE	April 6		Nothing special to record - preparing for tomorrow's march.	
	7		15th Divisional Route March - The Battalion paraded at 7 am. in company with the rest of the Brigade marched about 15 miles - The Battalion billets were in the village of TIPPEMONT, LE PLUDY, FLECHIN, BONCOURT - one Company in each - these villages are shown on the HAZEBROUCK sheet - 5A 1/100,000.	
	8		The 44th Brigade marched to the vicinity of ENGUINEGATTE in 1st Army Training Area & carried on attack practice. The country about 140 metres above sea level. Everything was very pleasant the day being very well spent. Returned to billets in ALLOUAGNE. men marching very well indeed, no men fell out.	
	9			
	10		A demonstration of a landing attack was made through country of rather batteries over broken. The 9th to flank watch of would render batteries over the demonstration. The rear of the Brigade looking on.	

WAR DIARY or INTELLIGENCE SUMMARY

Army Form C. 2118

Place	Date 1916	Hour	Summary of Events and Information	Remarks and references to Appendices
ALLOUAGNE	11 April		2 Lieut. C. V. Richardson granted an extension of leave on medical grounds to 17/5/16. Zeppelin Shows were taken in Turkey.	
	12		The Battalion went to the baths at AUCHEL today.	
	13		1st Army Routine Order No 342 dated 11th April 1916. No 5/0665 Pte J. BARKER 16th (S) Bn. The Gordon Highlanders. On 27/2/16 Pte. Barker with other men was engaged in unfuzing bombs when his fuze shield broke. He was talking hence visible to a defective striker, breaking into the bomb would explode. Pte. Barker showing fine valour dropped the bomb & shouted for cover saying that the bomb had fallen was a bomb which would probably explode. He ran back shielding ignited bomb away. Before Pte. Barker could regain cover the bomb exploded & he was seriously injured. His action probably prevented the other men being exploded on, although two other men were injured the action certainly prevented a more serious accident. The G.O.C. 1st Army wishes to express his appreciation of his act of courage & which will be noted in the Regimental Conduct Sheet of Pte Barker.	

Army Form C. 2118

WAR DIARY
or
INTELLIGENCE SUMMARY
(Erase heading not required.)

Instructions regarding War Diaries and Intelligence Summaries are contained in F. S. Regs., Part II. and the Staff Manual respectively. Title Pages will be prepared in manuscript.

Place	Date 1916	Hour	Summary of Events and Information	Remarks and references to Appendices
ALLOUAGNE	14 Ap.		A draft of 17 men arrived.	
	15 Ap.		Major A.K. LONGMAN returned to the Battalion for duty. Major A.W. ANGUS took over command of "L" Coy. from Capt. MOFFAT	
	16 Ap. Sunday		Church Services were held. Presbyterian 10.45 am. Church of England 11.45 am. Roto services being held in the Divisional Recreation Room. Roman Catholic Services in Parish Church at 11.45 am.	
	17 Ap.		Highland Brigade Games were to be held today, but as it rained very hard from 2 pm it was not possible to hold them again & as it rained every day for nearly a week. A draft of 18 arrived.	
	18 Ap.		Brigadier General F.J. MARSHALL took over command of the 46th Infantry Brigade today.	
	19 Ap.		Brigadier General M.G. WILKINSON C.B. M.V.O. left ALLOUAGNE – he had commanded the 46th Brigade since it was formed & was its first and only Brigadier to this date.	

1875   Wt. W593/826 1,000,000 4/15   J.B.C. & A.   A.D.S.S./Forms/C. 2118.

WAR DIARY
or
INTELLIGENCE SUMMARY

Army Form C. 2118

(Erase heading not required.)

Place	Date 1916	Hour	Summary of Events and Information	Remarks and references to Appendices
AUBIGNY	18 Ap.		The Pipe Band of the Battalion assembled to see him off & representatives of all Battalion lines the road & gave 3 cheers as he went.	
	19.20		Nothing special to record	
	21		The Battalion was inspected by the in C. 15th Division - a fine morning but not afternoon. Several of the Inspection was received and in forming row the men looked remarkably well. Attack on had taken place turnouts his line & table was as under:-	
		12.20	Bombing Squad "I" Coy.	
		3.45	Wiring " - " - "	
		4.30	1 Platoon " L " Coy. on Range to fire (1) a (company practice)	
		4.30	Lewis Gun Detachment	(2) a snapshot "
		5.30	3 Platoons " L " Coy. & marching order	(3) a fire control "
		5.45	"K" & "M" Coy. in drill order to carry out Company drill	

Army Form C. 2118

WAR DIARY
or
INTELLIGENCE SUMMARY
(Erase heading not required.)

Place	Date	Hour	Summary of Events and Information	Remarks and references to Appendices
ALLOUAGNE	1916 21 April		Report on 44th Highland Brigade, after inspection by G.O.C. 15th Division. The G.O.C. directs me to inform you that he is pleased with the drill, musketry, training & general turn out of your Brigade today. The course this morning was satisfactory in all matters observed from the last 3 weeks work in billets. In turn out of the 10th GORDON HIGHLANDERS has been very satisfactory in every particular. There are however certain points to which he wishes you to give your attention and must avoid being hidden & none should be approximated, consist in estimates. 1) nationals will be as fast as. (a) Wiring. (b) Musketry. The musketry training of the 8th Seaforth Highlanders requires attention. (c) Bombing. There practice in throwing is to get length in response. (d) In many cases web equipment has not been cleaned as has been ordered by the G.O.C. in several measures. There was responsible noticeable in the 7th Cameron Highlanders. (e) The depth of the 8th Seaforth Highlanders are in an indifferent state & require closer points. The G.O.C. however to your notice today during his inspection. (sd) H. KNOX Lieut. Col. General Staff. 15th Division.	
	21/4/16			

Army Form C. 2118

WAR DIARY
or
INTELLIGENCE SUMMARY
(Erase heading not required.)

Instructions regarding War Diaries and Intelligence Summaries are contained in F.S. Regs., Part II. and the Staff Manual respectively. Title Pages will be prepared in manuscript.

Place	Date 1916	Hour	Summary of Events and Information	Remarks and references to Appendices
ALLOUAGNE	21 April		2nd Lieut. A.K. FRIDAY joined for duty.	
	22		The whole Battalion was out for fatigue, filling in trenches that had been dug by some one else at GONNEHIEM and MT. BERNENCHON. Worked until noon all day and the men were issued extra footlers and were out 11 hours.	
	23 Easter Sunday		Church Parades. Presbyterians 10.45 am. Church of England 11.45 am. Roman Catholics 11 am in Parish Church. A new organisation had been decided on for Trench Warfare Battalions & 14/11 L.M. Battery consisting of 1. 4" mortar 2. 3" Stokes mortars 2. 3.7" mountain 10 "Garden Syke" & 7 "Canadian" rifles each Battalion finding 1 Officer. 1 Sergeant & Corpls. 16 Privates. Teams were to have turnover from each Battalion. The change of weather started today - the rain stopped & became hot however.	

Army Form C. 2118

WAR DIARY
or
INTELLIGENCE SUMMARY
(Erase heading not required.)

Place	Date	Hour	Summary of Events and Information	Remarks and references to Appendices
			Extract from Farewell order by General Wilkinson Cmdg. 44th Brigade dated 18/4/16.	
			"He is quite certain that the present high state of discipline will be maintained."	
			15th Division memo dated 17/4/16 — The Divisional Commander regrets ... the unchivalrous conduct of the troops under his command.	
			1st Corps Circular dated 7/4/16 — The discipline of the troops of hrs ... and 15th Divisions is very bad ...	
			44th Brigade dated 27/4/16 — The Brigadier (F.J. MARSHALL) makes us to reference to all ranks of the 44th Highland Brigade his appreciation of their steadiness & soldierly bearing during the trying ordeal of their ; twice fired hostile gas attack. He records impress on them his points. Firstly that "gas" is a deadly weapon with far reaching results, and secondly that all gas attacks can be truly overcome by coolness the invisible observance of the instructions which have been issued.	

WAR DIARY
or
INTELLIGENCE SUMMARY

Army Form C. 2118

Place	Date	Hour	Summary of Events and Information	Remarks and references to Appendices
April	19.16		Letter received from Association of Highland Societies of Edinburgh.	3 Eton Gardens, Edinburgh.

The D.C.
10 Gordon Highlanders.

Dear Sir,

At a meeting of the Association of the Highland Societies of Edinburgh held on Sunday 7th inst; it was unanimously agreed to convey to you the high appreciation felt by the Highland community of Edinburgh for the conspicuous part taken by the Highland Regiments during the present war. The bravery & endurance shown by the soldiers of these regiments in the present conflict has never been surpassed, and our Association takes pride in recording that the Highland regiments are still the very flower of the British Army.

I was instructed to convey to you the congratulations of the Association for the distinguished part played by the men under your command and to wish you & your men the best wishes of the Association for a safe & speedy victory.

(Signed) George Philip
Hon. Secy.

WAR DIARY or INTELLIGENCE SUMMARY

Army Form C. 2118

Place	Date 1916	Hour	Summary of Events and Information	Remarks and references to Appendices
ALLOUAGNE	24 Ap.		Major H.K. LONGMAN returned to Officers Training School at GOSNAY. Major A.W. ANGUS returned to acting 2nd in command of the Battalion. Capt. F.J.C. MOFFAT took over command of "L" Coy from Major ANGUS. Capt. A.P. BETHELL returned as instructor to Officers Training School at GOSNAY. "I" Coy. was taken over by Capt. PATERSON. Highland Games has been arranged for 17th April but has to be postponed on account of the rain. It had never been possible to hold them, as rain just was practically continuous for a week. The stay at ALLOUAGNE had been a very good one; lots of training had been done as the men had lots of football & generally speaking tramlines the inhabitants, as usual, were our best friends.	

Army Form C. 2118

WAR DIARY
or
INTELLIGENCE SUMMARY
(Erase heading not required.)

Instructions regarding War Diaries and Intelligence Summaries are contained in F. S. Regs, Part II. and the Staff Manual respectively. Title Pages will be prepared in manuscript.

Place	Date 1915	Hour	Summary of Events and Information	Remarks and references to Appendices
ALLOUAGNE to BETHUNE	April 25		The Battalion in company with the 9th Seaforth Highlanders left about 11.30 am & marched to LILLERS where they entrained & came as far as BETHUNE where they spent the night. The 10th Gordon Highlanders were billeted in the Orphanage. Band played in the BETHUNE Square at Retreat. 6 Pipers & 9 Drummers. Brigadier General A.W. BAIRD D.S.O. commanding 10th Brigade — also an officer of the 2nd Gordon Highlanders recommended 1 to 1st Gordon Highlanders for some mementos of France as was much interested.	
BETHUNE to NOYELLES	26 April		The 10th Brigade took over to Rifle Brigade Sector of the QUARRIES Sector & was distributed as under — Right subsector — 9th Black Watch Left " — 7th Cameron Highlanders Support — 8th Seaforth Highlanders — In Trenches Reserve — 10th Gordon Highlanders — 2 Coys. VERMELLES H. Qrs. 2 Coys. } NOYELLES	

Army Form C. 2118

WAR DIARY
or
INTELLIGENCE SUMMARY
(Erase heading not required.)

Instructions regarding War Diaries and Intelligence Summaries are contained in F.S. Regs., Part II. and the Staff Manual respectively. Title Pages will be prepared in manuscript.

Place	Date 1916	Hour	Summary of Events and Information	Remarks and references to Appendices
VERMELLES & NOYELLES	27 April		A German "gas" attack. — but it was never pushed home as the Battalion although in Brigade Reserve was not called out. Hostile shelling in VERMELLES started at 4 a.m. & was intense till 7 a.m. when & for some time later came over — but lasted about 3/4 hour now & in NOYELLES he also took his time to pare — hostile shelling throughout has now continued intermittently all morning — many "tear" shells were put over. There seemed to be more in front, as the enemy snipers are not good — the gas masks we believe is very good and complete protection. — two Coys in VERMELLES were busily employed in carrying up bombs — S.A.A. to the front line — otherwise the Battalion took no part. The inhabitants all had gas masks & got into houses & did not seem to mind.	

WAR DIARY
or
INTELLIGENCE SUMMARY
(Erase heading not required.)

Army Form C. 2118

Place	Date	Hour	Summary of Events and Information	Remarks and references to Appendices
VERMELLES NOEULLES	27 April 1916		The only casualty was the Padre attached to the Battalion. (Captain to Rev. H.B. St John de Vine) He was killed in VERMELLES about 100 yards from his dug out, which he had left large & see that the men were under cover or had their gas helmets ready. His end was a fitting one; he was forever looking after the men, helping all wounds and in the places of danger, always in the front line and generally distributing cigarettes. Never sparing himself, where his men were — there he was. The whole Battalion mourns his loss — he was loved by all — particularly by "I" Company, for some reason to he attached himself to them & lived with the Officers of that Company. He was killed in VERMELLES at the cross roads about 250 yards N.W. of the main Church — and he will be buried in the VERMELLES cemetery.	Rev. H.B. St John de Vine

W.W. Montgomery Lt. Colonel.
10th Gordon Highlanders

WAR DIARY or INTELLIGENCE SUMMARY

Army Form C. 2118

(Erase heading not required.)

Place	Date 1916	Hour	Summary of Events and Information	Remarks and references to Appendices
VERMELLES	27 April	p.m.	working parties as under were found –	
NOYELLES		2.0	2 N.C.O's & 40 men carrying explosives for 180th Tunnelling Coy. R.E.	
		5.0	1 " 10 " " " " " to O.G.1.	
			– gun ? – revetting Reserve	
		7.0	1 Officer & 60 other ranks under 74th Coy. R.E. at Bde. H.Q.	
		8.0	1 N.C.O. 15 men under 73rd Coy. R.E.	
		8.30	4 men pushing truck for T.M.B.	
		10.0	1 N.C.O. 10 men pushing truck into trench for T.M.B.	
		11.0	2 N.C.O's 20 men removing sandbags under 180th Coy. R.E.	
	28 Ap.	a.m.	working parties were found –	
		1.0	2 NCO's 20 men under R.E.	
		2.0	3 " 27 " " R.E.	
		7.0	2 Officers 50 O.R. on Support Trench	
		8.0	1 " 50 " carrying S.A.A. & Bombs.	
		7.0	1 " 60 " at Bde. H.Q.w.	
		10.30	1 " 60 " " " "	
		10.30	1 " 16 " under R.E.	

H. Clipsis

Army Form C. 2118.

WAR DIARY
or
INTELLIGENCE SUMMARY.
(Erase heading not required.)

Instructions regarding War Diaries and Intelligence Summaries are contained in F. S. Regs., Part II. and the Staff Manual respectively. Title pages will be prepared in manuscript.

Place	Date 1915	Hour	Summary of Events and Information	Remarks and references to Appendices
VERMELLES	28 Sept	7 pm	Capt. the Rev. H.B. St John de Vine was buried in the VERMELLES Cemetery - his service was conducted by Colonel & the Rev. BLACKBURN - Senior Church of England chaplain 1st Corps. Representation from each Coy. in the Battalion among others was present.	
VERMELLES	29 Sept	9 pm	A gas alarm at night received by the Division on our right attacking.	
NOEULLES	29 Sept	3.45 am	Hostile gas attack on the Battalion in reserve about to, but were not rallied out the gas didn't reach them - Firing ceased about 5.15 a.m.	
	30 Sept		10th Gordon Highlanders relieve 7th Cameron Highlanders in front line.	

T.134. Wt. W708-776. 500000. 4/15. Sir J. C. & S.

Army Form C. 2118.

WAR DIARY
or
INTELLIGENCE SUMMARY.
(Erase heading not required.)

Instructions regarding War Diaries and Intelligence Summaries are contained in F. S. Regs., Part II. and the Staff Manual respectively. Title pages will be prepared in manuscript.

Place	Date 1916	Hour	Summary of Events and Information	Remarks and references to Appendices
VERMELLES	29 Ap.	8.0 a.m.	1 N.C.O. & 1 man carrying influenza	
NOYELLES		9.30	1 — 9.50 men — do —	
		9.30	1 — 12 — fm T.M.B.	
			1 Officer 25 — carrying up stores to forward dump.	
TRENCHES	30. Ap. Sunday		Relieved 7th Cameron Highlanders in left subsection QUARRIES Sector. On our right were the 9th Seaforth Highlanders & on our left the 7th K.O.S.B's. The relief went off alright, beginning at 9.20 a.m. it was completed by 12 noon. HULLUCH ALLEY up which L. Coy. went came in for a good deal of shelling, but there were no casualties, although one shell dropped in the trench just in front of them. The day was quiet, wet and cold, usual shelling in activity of any kind. The Battalion frontage extended from SOUTHERN JUNCTION of SWINBOURNE LOOP and BROOKWOOD TRENCH (inclusive) to New RIFLEMAN'S ALLEY (inclusive) and Headquarters at P.C. G10 d 4.3. in BRESLAU AVENUE. The 4/1 L.M. BATTERY is in the left subsection.	

W. Macpherson Lt Col.
1st Gordon Highlanders

Vol 10
XV
10 factors

Army Form C. 2118.

WAR DIARY or INTELLIGENCE SUMMARY.
(Erase heading not required.)

Instructions regarding War Diaries and Intelligence Summaries are contained in F. S. Regs., Part II. and the Staff Manual respectively. Title pages will be prepared in manuscript.

Place	Date	Hour	11/2/16-13/2/16		14/2/16-21/2/16				Summary of Events and Information	Remarks and references to Appendices
			O.	O.R.	O.	O.R.	O.	O.R.		
Killed in action			-	5	0	2	0	2		
Wounded	"		-	18	0	7	0	19		
" (at duty)			-	-	0	4	0	1		
Sent to Hospital			3	60	1	33	1	72		
Total			3	83	1	46	1	93		
Returned from hosp.	10			3				11		
from wounded	3		13	4		7				
Total loss			3	70	1	33	1	82		

Army Form C. 2118.

Instructions regarding War Diaries and Intelligence Summaries are contained in F. S. Regs., Part II. and the Staff Manual respectively. Title pages will be prepared in manuscript.

WAR DIARY
or
INTELLIGENCE SUMMARY.
(Erase heading not required.)

Place	Date 1916	Hour	Summary of Events and Information	Remarks and references to Appendices
April			Casualties during month — Killed 1 Officer (attached - C. of E. Chaplain)	
			Died of wounds 1	
			Wounded 4	
			1 (attached 186th Cy R.E.)	
			— (at duty) 1	
			Died in hospital 2	
			(from illness) —	
			9	
			Sent to Hospital —	
			2 Officers 50 Other ranks	
			Returns 13 — —	
			Drafts in 3" — 6	
			14 — 17	
			17 — 18	
			20 — 1	
			30 — 11	
			— 63	
			Transfers from 9th G.H. 1	
			64	
			Officers joining — 2nd Lt. A.K. PRIDAY 21.4.16	
			Lt. L.G. ROBERTSON 17.4.16	
			O.C. F. ELLIOT 11.4.16	
			Invalided to England -	
			Struck off strength Lt. J.H. SEMPLE	

10th (S) Bn. Gordon Highlanders

War Diary

1st to 12th May 1916

From,
　　Officer Commanding
　　　11th Entrenching Battalion.

To,
　　　Officer i/c
　　　A.G's Office.
　　　　Base.

　　　　Herewith War Diary of 10th
Bn.Gordon Highlanders from 1st to 12th
May 1916.

　　　　　　　　　　　Major
　　　　Commanding 11th Entrenching Bn.
　　　　(Late O.C.10th Bn.Gordon Highlrs.

5th June 1916.

Army Form C. 2118.

WAR DIARY
or
INTELLIGENCE SUMMARY.
(Erase heading not required.)

Instructions regarding War Diaries and Intelligence Summaries are contained in F.S. Regs., Part II. and the Staff Manual respectively. Title pages will be prepared in manuscript.

XV Corps / Wadgchy 13th May 1916
See p. 10 of General
Recd 11 Ent W.D vol 115

Place	Date 1916	Hour	Summary of Events and Information	Remarks and references to Appendices
TRENCHES	11 May		Patrols of the three Coys. in the Rising Sun were out last night. Shrapnel had useful information. One of the HAIRPIN Craters was reported as 60 feet deep. "I" Coy on the right had a very quiet time. "K" — in centre was bombed with rifle grenades & these caused doubt, but retaliated vigorously on in the red gaps the upper hand, sending back a continuous stream of rifle grenades & trench mortar bombs. At night the Lewis gunners Rifle Grenade Saps were dug out & deepened. "L" Coy on the left had a warm time. Their trench was bombarded with 5.9's from 1 p.m. to 2.30 p.m. and ceperforated with batteries. There was blame in her place & also to the Kurrane & RABBIT RUN, but there were no casual ties. Enemy sent over small smoke bombs but they did not ignite. Enemy put up two red lights. Bombardn hit front support line with heavy trench mortars & rifle grenades.	
		6.20 pm		
		7.0		
		9.5	Our Artillery helped by retaliation for red bombardment. Just about ten lives were a false gas alarm.	

T.134. Wt. W708—776. 500000. 4/15. Sir J.C. & S.

WAR DIARY
or
INTELLIGENCE SUMMARY

Army Form C. 2118.

Place	Date 1916	Hour	Summary of Events and Information	Remarks and references to Appendices
TRENCHES	2 May		"I" Coy. dug 50 yards connecting trench. Wherever our work received fire, the Germans were heard by whistles, which can be distinctly heard.	
			"K" Coy. commenced wiring base of HAIRPIN. This was much hindered by hostile grenades & trench mortars. Our snipers had some very good shots.	
		3.19 am	7.L. & S.F.T. of left company shelled by 5.9's. No casualties, but F.L. blown in in two places.	
		4.45	No place on C.T. known as RABBIT RUN was also blown in in two places.	
			"I" Coy. in night had a quiet time only a few trench mortar bombs & grenades.	

WAR DIARY
or
INTELLIGENCE SUMMARY.

(Erase heading not required.)

Army Form C. 2118.

Instructions regarding War Diaries and Intelligence Summaries are contained in F. S. Regs., Part II. and the Staff Manual respectively. Title pages will be prepared in manuscript.

Place	Date	Hour	Summary of Events and Information	Remarks and references to Appendices
	1916			
TRENCHES	3 May	12.30 am	About midnight 2/3 enemy made small bombing attack on centre sap of HARDIN, but it was not pushed home.	
		2.0 am	Battalion Headquarters attacked enemy; it shelled by 5.9 shrapnel about 2 pm. only one direct hit on the trench was obtained and ten wounded 4 men one of whom died subsequently.	
		1.45 am	A false gas alarm, all troops stood to in ten minutes or one minute somewhat the alarm unjustly. Every part of the subsection was bombarded with 5.9, H.E. Shrapnel, Whizzbangs, aerial darts attached mortars. but only one man was touched besides those wounded H. Run nothing. I died of wounds 2-5 men in all. A shell nearly went down the entrance to "D" Coy dug out & luckily most of their men crouching. 2 Lt. N.E. SPROTT has a marvellous escape, a shell just...	

T.134. W1. W708-776. 500000. 4/15. Six J. C. & S.

Army Form C. 2118.

WAR DIARY
or
INTELLIGENCE SUMMARY.
(Erase heading not required.)

Place	Date 1916	Hour	Summary of Events and Information	Remarks and references to Appendices
TRENCHES 4th A.	May 4th		Relieved the 7th Cameron Highlanders in the Firing line and the latter moved back into Brigade Support in the O.B.'s & CURLEY CRESCENT. The relief was completed by 12 noon. Everything working smoothly.	
		7pm	A big mine was blown up by us, which considerably altered the features of the HAIRPIN SAPS, and was successful in destroying enemy galleries – beyond carrying up ammunition thanks to Battalion were not required to help.	
			While the Battalion was in Brigade Support the following working parties were found daily.	
		9.0 am	24 men at sail line to work } under 73rd Co. R.E.	
		1.0 pm		
		5.0 pm		
		9.0 am	making dug outs. } 2/Lt N.C.D's & } Working under 130th Tunnelling	
		1.0 pm	} 140 men } Co. R.E.	
		5.0 pm		
		5 pm		
		11 pm		
		10 pm	} 1 N.C.O. & 20 men for which number	
		4 am	} 253 " " Co. R.E.	
		10 pm	20 men to carry T.M. Bombs to front line.	

Army Form C. 2118.

WAR DIARY
or
INTELLIGENCE SUMMARY.

(Erase heading not required.)

Instructions regarding War Diaries and Intelligence
Summaries are contained in F. S. Regs., Part II.
and the Staff Manual respectively. Title pages
will be prepared in manuscript.

Place	Date	Hour	Summary of Events and Information	Remarks and references to Appendices
	1916			
TRENCHES	5 Aug		D.B.1 shelled with 5.9 between 9 & 10 am. - determining his Battalion was not invited.	
" "	6 Aug		2Lt. J. SMITH joined for duty even posted to "K" Coy. The Rev. A.K. CORNISH Chaplain to the Forces joined the Battalion	

T./134. Wt. W708-776. 500000. 4/15. Sir J. C. & S.

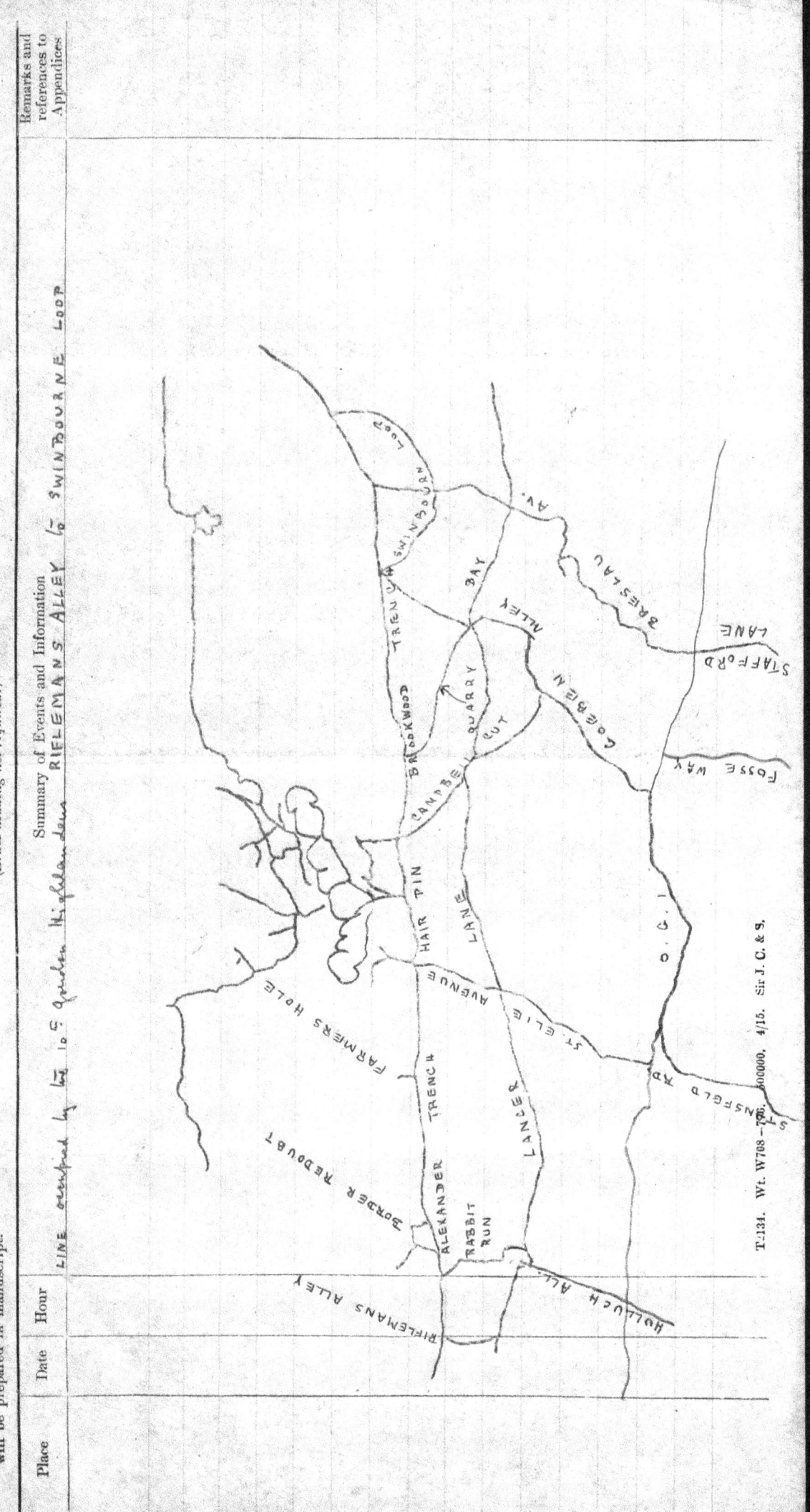

Army Form C. 2118.

WAR DIARY
or
INTELLIGENCE SUMMARY.
(Erase heading not required.)

Instructions regarding War Diaries and Intelligence Summaries are contained in F. S. Regs., Part II. and the Staff Manual respectively. Title pages will be prepared in manuscript.

Place	Date 1916	Hour	Summary of Events and Information	Remarks and references to Appendices
TRENCHES Sunday	7 May		HULLUCH ALLEY and O.B.1 was heavily shelled by 5.9 between 9 am & 12 noon — one man was killed and one wounded. HULLUCH ALLEY and STANSFELD ROAD were both knocked in by shells — the latter was repaired by Volunteers from R.A.M.C. headed by Captain E.A. LUMLEY R.A.M.C. Definite news was received that the 8th & 910th Battalions GORDON HIGHLANDERS were to be amalgamated at an early date.	
—"—	8 May		The Battalion moved up from Brigade Support & relieved the 7th Cameron Highlanders in the Left Subsection QUARRY Section, the relief worked very smoothly was completed by 11.0 pm. The 7th Cameron Highlanders moved into Brigade Support. The 8th Seaforth Highlanders relieved the 9th Black Watch in the Right Subsection QUARRY Section. A cold day with a S.W. wind very strong. The day was materially quiet, although the front lots were billiard on trenches held by M Coy and 1 man was killed & about 4 wounded.	

T.134. Wt. W708-776. 500000. 4/15. Sir J. C. & S.

WAR DIARY
or
INTELLIGENCE SUMMARY.
(Erase heading not required.)

Place	Date 1916	Hour	Summary of Events and Information	Remarks and references to Appendices
TRENCHES	8 May		The position of Companies in the line was	
			"L" commanded by Captain PATERSON — Havrincourt	
			"K" — " — Lieut. F.W. GORDON — Cartier — Right.	
			"L" — " — " RIDDEL — " — " — K	
			"M" — " — Captain LONGMAN — Reserve	
			Captain MOFFAT at a Machine Gun Course — Captain THOM on leave — "L"	
	9 May		A quiet day — some shelling of our trenches, interrupting services. We expended a Trench Mortar & Rifle Grenade Strafe at 8 a.m. in the morning. Thin drew retaliation — but it was a windy day & observation difficult. At night-shewit. J. COLLIER was wounded in the leg by a rifle grenade, which dropped at his feet. A little rain making the trenches muddy & worse.	

Army Form C. 2118.

WAR DIARY
or
INTELLIGENCE SUMMARY.
(Erase heading not required.)

Instructions regarding War Diaries and Intelligence Summaries are contained in F. S. Regs., Part II. and the Staff Manual respectively. Title pages will be prepared in manuscript.

Place	Date 1916	Hour	Summary of Events and Information	Remarks and references to Appendices
TRENCHES	10 May		The early morning rifle grenade stretch rather slight commenced at 4.30 am finished at 5 am. There was rather more persistent heavier trench mortar firing than usual during the day there was a good deal of shelling, especially on BRESLAU AVENUE where the Germans were evidently trying to get a trench mortar position.	

Army Form C. 2118

WAR DIARY
or
INTELLIGENCE SUMMARY

(Erase heading not required.)

Instructions regarding War Diaries and Intelligence Summaries are contained in F. S. Regs., Part II. and the Staff Manual respectively. Title Pages will be prepared in manuscript.

Place	Date	Hour	Summary of Events and Information	Remarks and references to Appendices

1875 Wt. W 593/826 1,000,000 4/15 I.B.C. & A. A.D.S.S./Forms/C. 2118.

Army Form C. 2118.

WAR DIARY
or
INTELLIGENCE SUMMARY.
(Erase heading not required.)

Instructions regarding War Diaries and Intelligence Summaries are contained in F. S. Regs., Part II. and the Staff Manual respectively. Title pages will be prepared in manuscript.

Place	Date 1916	Hour	Summary of Events and Information	Remarks and references to Appendices
TRENCHES & BETHUNE	11 May		The 44th Brigade was relieved in the line by the 6th Brigade. The 10th Gordon Highlanders being relieved by the 10th Scottish Rifles. The relief commenced about 10.15 am, finishing very smoothly has over object — not a shell being fired. The 10th Gordon Highrs. halted for a meal at SAILLY LABOURSE and then marched on into billets at BETHUNE. The Pipe Band played in the Town Square at intervals.	
		5.30 pm	Orders received to stand to — and be ready to move at once.	
		7.0/15	Battalion moved out into NOEUX LES MINES road preparatory to entraining — but orders were cancelled & Battalion moved back into billets & were not moved out again that night. The Germans had attacked the HOHENZOLLERN REDOUBT starting a heavy bombardment at 3.15 pm (just as the H.Qrs. 44th Brigade left, handing over to 6th Brigade) (in withdrawing trenches in RIFLEMANS ALLEY where the 10th Gordons Highlanders had reached in the beginning) (the 10th Gordon Highlanders had reached in the beginning)	

T.134. Wt. W708-776. 500000. 4/15. Sir J.C. & S.

WAR DIARY or INTELLIGENCE SUMMARY

Place	Date 1916	Hour	Summary of Events and Information	Remarks and references to Appendices
BETHUNE	12 May		The 8th, 9th & 10th (Service) Battalions were amalgamated and the surplus men were sent to the 11th Entrenching Battalion which was formed at BETHUNE. The new Battalion to Gordon Highlanders was commanded by Lieut Col H.P. BURN. The new " " 9th " " " " W.W. MACGREGOR. The new " " 11th Entrenching Battalion " " " F.J.E. MOFFAT. In amalgamating the 8th & 10th Batts. Gordon Highlanders the system adopted was that two companies of each Battalion were taken make up to full strength of officers & men and thus the two Battalions formed one. The 10th Battalion Companies retained were "K" which commanded by Capt. J.C. THOM and these became "C" & "D" Coy respectively in the 8th Battalion. The 8th Battalion having handed over its equipment etc a somewhat African Battalion on leaving the 9th Division. The 10th Battalion were handed with every kit of equipment (except riding horses) and these were all taken over by the 8th Battalion. The amalgamation was completed over today.	

WAR DIARY
or
INTELLIGENCE SUMMARY.
(Erase heading not required.)

Army Form C. 2118.

Place	Date	Hour	Summary of Events and Information	Remarks and references to Appendices
BETHUNE			The following Officers were transferred to the amalgamated 8/10 Battalion.	
			Captain J. G. THOM Captain J. G. MOFFAT	
			Lieut. J. B. WOOD Captain L. G. ROBERTSON	
			2 " A. N. BAIN 2 " R. M. RIDDEL	
			" A. F. SPROTT " R. A. M. BLACK	
			" A. K. PRIDAY " H. L. KNOWLES	
			" JACKSON	
			Reserve Officers — Lieut. C. G. HARPER Transport Officer	
			2 " O. ELLIOT	
			" J. SMITH	
			The following attached Officers were also transferred:-	
			Major H. R. LONGMAN (Commandant of Divisional School, GOSNAY)	
			Capt. A. P. L. BETHEL (Instructor — do —) 15th	
			Lieut. A. INGLIS (44th Brigade Bombing School Instructor)	
			Capt. E. A. LUMLEY R.A.V.C.	
			Capt. Rev. H. K. CORNISH, C.F.	

Casualties during last tour in trenches. 25/4/16 to 1/5/16
Killed   1 Officer (Capt. Lt Rev. H.S.J. de VINE C.F.)
    "   3 men   0.R.
Wounded   1 Officer   Total   2   26
           22 men   2   22
                                   —   —
Died of wounds 1 man   2   48
Sick to Hospital 20   R.T.A.   4
Shell shock   2   ——   ——
                  ——   2   44
                                          ══   ══

Strength of battalion before Amalgamation
   Officers   33   Other Ranks   848
   Attached   2
                 ——
                 35

Alstrup, Major
for Lt Colonel 13th Border Highlanders

WAR DIARY
or
INTELLIGENCE SUMMARY
(Erase heading not required.)

Army Form C. 2118

Instructions regarding War Diaries and Intelligence Summaries are contained in F. S. Regs, Part II. and the Staff Manual respectively. Title Pages will be prepared in manuscript.

Place	Date	Hour	Summary of Events and Information	Remarks and references to Appendices
	1915			
September			List of presents received by the Battalion	
			Queen Alexandria Field Force Fund	11 bales comforts
			Lord Provosts comforts Committee - Edinburgh	Socks & Vermin powder
			Overseas Club - through Gazetin, Piccadilly	Tobacco cigarettes
			Hillhead High School, Glasgow	9000 cigarettes
			Scholars 3 George Street School	cigarettes, mouthing paper
October			Overseas Club - through Martin, Piccadilly	Tobacco cigarettes
			Lord Provosts Committee - Edinburgh	30 pair socks
			Overseas Club - through Martin, Piccadilly	Tobacco cigarettes
November			Overseas Club - through Martin, Piccadilly	Tobacco cigarettes

WAR DIARY
or
INTELLIGENCE SUMMARY

Army Form C. 2118

Place	Date	Hour	Summary of Events and Information	Remarks and references to Appendices
	1915			
December			Miss Scott Moncrieff	Cigarettes
			Miss Farquharson	Mittens
			County of Aberdeen	Plum puddings
	1916			
January			Miss Farquharson	8 prs. Socks / 114 - Mitts / 78 Mufflers
			Lord Provost's Committee - Edinburgh	92 prs. Socks / 6 Shirts
February			Lord Provost's Committee - Edinburgh	Cigarettes / 36 prs. Socks / 85 - Mitts / 30 Mufflers / 6 hoslen helmets / Cigarettes / 1 parcel Books

Army Form C. 2118

WAR DIARY
or
INTELLIGENCE SUMMARY
(Erase heading not required.)

Instructions regarding War Diaries and Intelligence Summaries are contained in F. S. Regs., Part II. and the Staff Manual respectively. Title Pages will be prepared in manuscript.

Place	Date	Hour	Summary of Events and Information	Remarks and references to Appendices
February	1916		Scottish Trish Black Tobacco Fund "Princess Office" Kouilles for John Robertson	20 lbs Tobacco 1 lb. Cigarettes
			Mrs John Robertson	Brooks for Pyjamas
			Sir Ronald Stewart	50 pairs Socks
March			Daily Express Fund for H.M.S. Forces from various donors	12 roots sugar 10 books
			Lint Proposati Committee - Shirburn of	10 pr Socks
			County of Aberdeen Sea Work Association	200 pair Socks 50 Shirts
			Mrs Henry Loungman	2 pounds disinfecting soap

1875. Wt. W593/826 1,000,000 4/15 T.B.C. & A. A.D.S.S./Forms/C. 2118.

Army Form C. 2118.

WAR DIARY
or
INTELLIGENCE SUMMARY.
(Erase heading not required.)

Instructions regarding War Diaries and Intelligence Summaries are contained in F. S. Regs., Part II. and the Staff Manual respectively. Title pages will be prepared in manuscript.

Place	Date	Hour	Summary of Events and Information	Remarks and references to Appendices
	1916			
March			Sir David Stewart — Boundary House	50 pairs socks
			Airdrie New Monkland & Airdrie Central Assoc. for Relief Xmas	130 — do —
			Lord Provost's Committee — Edinburgh	22 — do —
			— do —	6 Shirts
April			William McKinnell — Scottish Thaw Fund Svg.	12 Chs. Tobacco
			Unison Officers — Hamilton	
			County of Aberdeen — War Supply Assn.	300 pairs socks
			Daily Express Universal Fund — various donors	12 revolver ???

www.ingramcontent.com/pod-product-compliance
Lightning Source LLC
Chambersburg PA
CBHW081401160426
43193CB00013B/2083